A School District's
— *Journey to* —
EXCELLENCE

Dedicated to the school board members, administrators, teachers, and employees of the Wake County Public School System who helped us and our wives provide our children with excellent K–12 educations, and to all those Wake County business people who give of their time and expertise to enhance education.

—Bill McNeal and Tom Oxholm

A School District's
Journey to
EXCELLENCE

Lessons From Business and Education

BILL McNEAL ❧ TOM OXHOLM

Foreword by Jim Hunt
Former Governor, North Carolina

**CORWIN
PRESS**
A SAGE Company

For information:

Corwin Press
A SAGE Company
2455 Teller Road
Thousand Oaks, California 91320
www.corwinpress.com

SAGE Ltd.
1 Oliver's Yard
55 City Road
London EC1Y 1SP
United Kingdom

SAGE India Pvt. Ltd.
B 1/I 1 Mohan Cooperative
    Industrial Area
Mathura Road, New Delhi 110 044
India

SAGE Asia-Pacific Pte. Ltd.
33 Pekin Street #02-01
Far East Square
Singapore 048763

Printed in the United States of America.

Library of Congress Cataloging-in-Publication Data

McNeal, Bill.
A school district's journey to excellence: lessons from business and education /
Bill McNeal, Tom Oxholm.
     p. cm.
Includes bibliographical references and index.
ISBN 978-1-4129-4157-0 (cloth: acid-free paper)
ISBN 978-1-4129-4158-7 (pbk.: acid-free paper)
    1. Academic achievement—United States—Evaluation. 2. Educational tests and measurements—United States. 3. Education—United States—Evaluation. 4. Community and school—United States. I. Oxholm, Tom. II. Title.

LB1062.6.M435 2009
371.2'07—dc22   2008019165

This book is printed on acid-free paper.

08   09   10   11   12   10 9 8 7 6 5 4 3 2 1

Acquisitions Editor:	Arnis Burvikovs
Editorial Assistant:	Irina Dragut
Production Editor:	Eric Garner
Copy Editor:	Gretchen Treadwell
Typesetter:	C&M Digitals (P) Ltd.
Proofreader:	Theresa Kay
Indexer:	Terri Corry
Cover Designer:	Michael Dubowe

Contents

Foreword

Governor Jim Hunt

The Wake County Public School System is among the best in the nation, in large part because of many decades of great leadership by some courageous school board members and educators in the district, and great support from community and business people in the county. Bill McNeal and Tom Oxholm led powerfully in this tradition during their tenure with the school district. This book provides an insider's perspective on many of the challenges they faced and the successes they experienced.

Elsewhere, I have described five goals in North Carolina that we have to reach to make our schools the best in the nation: A Smart Start, Excellent Teaching, Safe Schools, High Student Performance, and Community Support. Every child should start school, on day one, healthy and ready to learn; every teacher should be committed to excellence; every school should be a safe and inviting place in which to learn; every student should be challenged to meet high standards; and every community should stand in support of its public schools. As you read this book, you will see how the Wake County Public School System has incorporated these same goals. The school district's Goal 2003 and Goal 2008 are the embodiment of the single-minded focus on excellence in education that we must have if we are to be the best in the nation—and if our nation is to remain the best in the world.

I have known Bill and his wife for many years and count them among my personal friends. What you should understand about Bill McNeal's use of the *Wizard of Oz* metaphor is that he truly believes in the principles of courage, brains, heart, and home. Watching Bill's career unfold over the years, it is evident to me that he is first and foremost a leader—a leader who chooses to exercise his talents in service and the field of public education. For this, students in Wake County, North Carolina, and, indeed, the nation, can be thankful. I don't know Tom Oxholm personally but I do know him by reputation; he is clearly a risk taker whose value system is deeply rooted in fairness and what's best for every child. The time he served as a member of the Wake County Board of Education is indeed a "profile in courage."

You will find Bill and Tom's book both enjoyable and educational. There are stories and lessons in the book that everyone can learn from, regardless of how you see yourself as a leader. I have always had a vision of how teachers can teach well, how students can learn, and how we can have successful schools where all students are safe, nurtured, and experience a culture where they are expected to do well. The standards that Bill and Tom emphasize—courage, brains, heart, and home—reflect this vision and should be the standards by which we all measure ourselves.

—Jim Hunt
Governor of North Carolina
1977–1985 and 1993–2001

Preface

This book is about courage, brains, heart, and home—four assets that are essential to carrying out the business of education. In this opening sentence, we mention these four assets and introduce one phrase—the business of education. In the chapters that follow, we will discuss how these four assets are each important to successfully educate the children and youth of our nation's public schools. And, we will argue that educational leaders must become adept at employing business practices and procedures in this endeavor.

Rightfully, there is a growing concern that public education in America may not be up to the challenge of preparing our children and youth for the economic competition that will develop among nations in the twenty-first century. To their credit, the American news media are doing their part by shining a light on this issue. Further, the American public is becoming increasingly aware of the issue, and there is a developing clamor for higher standards and greater accountability in public education. We maintain that this accountability requires educational leaders across the nation to look in the mirror and view their images differently so as to better inform and engage the public in the intricate business of schooling. The quality of life and the economic vitality of our neighborhoods, our communities, and our nation are tethered to the academic performance of students in our schools. We must get better at the business of education.

Toward this end, we worked side by side for thirteen years in the Wake County Public School System. During this period, the school district made significant gains on a variety of student outcome indicators and received numerous national accolades. In 2004, Bill was named National Superintendent of the Year by the American Association of School Administrators, and the district was recognized by *Forbes* magazine as the third best educational system among the biggest cities.

Our paths first crossed in 1994, when Tom was appointed to the Wake County Commissioner Task Force on Spending to be in charge of the education subcommittee (the largest section of the county's budget). Tom approached this experience with a good measure of an accountant's skepticism and Bill was his main contact with the school system. At the end of several months and hundreds of hours of studying the books, Tom emerged as a supporter of how the school system was spending citizens' tax dollars. Bill's open-book approach to information was a key factor in their ability to work together.

In 1994, Bill and Tom with many others organized the Business Education Leadership Council, which has become the main way business people in Wake County help teachers and students improve the educational process—a vehicle for businesses to support the school system without asking for money from them. Tom recently retired from this organization, now consisting of hundreds of businesses, and its unique way of operating will be explained in the book. The two joined forces again in 1995 when Bill, then associate superintendent, recognized the critical need for business collaboration to achieve success in implementing a federal School-to-Work Program. Bill called on Tom and other business leaders to not only participate, but also to lead the process. In 1998, Tom was named Wake County's Friend of Education for his work in strengthening school and business relationships. Tom also served a four-year term on the Wake County Board of Education (1999–2003). Selecting a new superintendent came up in the first six months of that term and the board chose Bill.

In this book, we describe the successes and challenges the school district has had in the past decade. During this period, the school district gained national recognition for the quality of its educational program. What is especially notable about this success is that it has been achieved in a countywide district that covers 864 square miles, has grown by 3,000 to 7,500 new students every year since the mid-1980s, has approximately 14 percent of children with special needs, is seeing dramatic growth in its population of students with limited English speaking skills, and spends less per student than most similarly-sized school systems. How has the district achieved impressive, jaw-dropping success in the face of the many challenges brought on by unrelenting enrollment growth and a period in our nation's history when public education is struggling? This book is written to address this question, and we will share our knowledge of the ways and means by which the school district is making continuous improvement to this already impressive measure of success.

The book is also written to allow other systems, large and small, to borrow from what we have done to achieve similar success. At the end of each chapter, we have provided a bulleted list of things you might do to improve operations in your district and schools. Certainly, you are already doing many of these things, and there are many other ways of bringing about improvements. Still, hopefully, a couple of our ideas will be new for you, or present a different perspective on a problem you are dealing with.

Finally, the book is written to describe how business practices and procedures can be applied in an educational environment to produce significant and sustainable gains. For too long, educators and business leaders have kept each other at arm's length. In times past, when business leaders have expressed their desire to help advance public education, education leaders have often sought to translate this expression into donations of money and products. But we need to rethink this position, because what we lose if we only seek money are the great practices and procedures that have helped make American businesses successful. These same practices and procedures could be adapted and adopted in public education.

When education leaders in the Wake County Public School System started listening to business leaders and employing business practices and procedures, significant positive changes resulted: test scores went up greatly, teacher satisfaction and retention improved, and community support for the schools reached new levels of satisfaction and pride. The following indicators represent selected statistics of interest to the public and provide examples of some of the most notable successes the school district achieved over ten school years.

Wake County Public School System[1]	*1993–94*	*2002–03*
Total student population	76,731	108,970
Free and reduced-price lunch students	17,679	26,526
Special education students	9,430	16,418
English as second language students	no records	5,179
Number of teachers	4,650	7,254
Number of schools	93	127
Tax dollars spent per student on operations	$4,470	$6,613
Average SAT score	1030	1067
Percent of high school students taking SAT	75	80
Advanced Placement scores (% scoring a 3 or higher)	77.8	78.6
Percent of students in Grades 3–8 at or above grade level on state End-of-Grade tests	75.7	91.3
Percent of high school students at or above grade level on state End-of-Course tests	73.5	83.2
Percent of students above grade level (Level IV)	47.4	60.4
Dropout rate (Grades 7–12)	4.3	1.8
Achievement gap (percentage points)	37.8	18.3

ORGANIZATION OF THIS BOOK

We have organized our book around four central themes from L. Frank Baum's *The Wonderful Wizard of Oz*, focusing on the assets of courage, brains, heart, and home. Who does not know of the Cowardly

Lion's search for courage, the Scarecrow's wish for a brain, the Tin Woodman's desire for a heart, and Dorothy's yearning to return home? In his six years as superintendent of the Wake County Public School System, Bill emphasized these assets in his interactions with thousands of teachers, parents, and community leaders. In many of his presentations, he delivered his message wrapped in these attributes. Bill maintains these assets are especially applicable to the business of education, and he knows they resonate with the public. Further, when speaking before groups, Bill knows how important it is to leave listeners with something to take with them when they exit. In this book, we develop our message regarding courage, brains, heart, and home; show how they relate to the business of education; and leave you with a challenge to put these assets into practice. When appropriately applied, these four assets are the keys to success for a classroom, school, or school district, and students will succeed academically, socially, and emotionally.

Courage is the willingness to do the right thing even though it may be more popular or politically expedient to do otherwise. In public education, courage is putting children first. It is about doing things differently than they have been done before—putting your career on the line by your commitment. And doing the right thing not because a researcher thinks it should work better, but because it is the right thing to do for children. Our section in Chapter 2, "Communicating With Your Public," describes a challenging time when school district leaders needed to demonstrate considerable courage while conducting an investigation into a case of fraud.

Brains demonstrate the capacity to continuously improve, resulting in life-long learning. By brains, we do not mean the work of the brain in learning; rather, we mean administrators using their brains to lock in continuous improvement as an expectation and measure of success. In this chapter of the book (Chapter 3), we emphasize the central role of planning and data analyses. The section on "Goal Setting and Planning" addresses something every school district does, and explains how the Wake County Public School System has approached setting goals for the district. Setting "Goal 2003" in the district changed our system forever and led to changes in the thinking of our employees and community. The section "Dollars and Sense" is about taking big dollar amounts and making common sense of spending practices. Explaining an $800 million budget to a skeptical audience in thirty minutes or saving dollars by taking a different approach to control escalating insurance costs are business practices that school systems can use. We have had to exercise our brains in new and novel ways with establishing educational goals and developing budgets for the school district.

Heart demonstrates the emotion of caring for others: students, parents, and staff. This chapter (Chapter 4) is about wanting the best for everyone and not accepting the usual answer of "There is not enough money." The section titled "Students Matter Most" is not an essay on the intricacies of the federal No Child Left Behind legislation. We don't need federal legislation to close the achievement gap. We know that we can close the achievement gap and accelerate all students; it takes heart to dedicate oneself to the effort. The section "Teachers Matter Most" is not a lobbying effort by the National Association of Educators for more pay. Teachers need incentives to improve their skills just like business workers, and knowing that somebody cares about their welfare makes their jobs better. It takes heart to care for every child, every parent, and every staff member.

Home is a place we all love and where we are loved unconditionally. It's a place where there is a feeling that one is nurtured and cared for by those who are in charge. That's what home should be for everyone, and in the absence of that for some, our schools must fill the void. When a student, teacher, or parent walks into a school building, he or she should feel just as comfortable and loved as in their own home. This can only come through major change in the way schools interact with their communities. In this last chapter of the book, we seek to "bring it all home" through indicating how courage, brains, and heart are essentially different aspects of the same value system, and it is this value system that undergirds the leader's ability to create a home-away-from-home at school for every child.

What is interesting about courage, brains, and heart and their relevance to public education—just as with the *Oz* lead characters—is that the characters in public education (students, parents, staff, and administrators) are also searching for something they already have. Every school system has the assets of which we write; these assets only need to be encouraged and supported. Wake County has been able to recognize these assets and nurture them to make a big difference in the lives of many. We have done this with the help of many wizards—ordinary people who make extraordinary things happen like in the classic tale of Oz.

There can be no doubt in your mind that we have a passion for improving public education. Further, we both believe that modern business concepts have made a huge difference in the education offered to students in Wake County, North Carolina. And, we are certain that other districts can make use of the same practices. Our hope is that this book helps you to further develop your courage, brains, heart, and sense of home for the purpose of contributing to educational improvement throughout the country.

Lastly, a few comments on our writing style are in order. Generally, we write in the third person, using terms such as "school district leaders," the "parents," or "the individual hired for this position." Most of what we have to say in this book is about others in our school district who have contributed to making the district as great as it is. Occasionally, we write about each other. Bill (McNeal) will write about something Tom said or did, and Tom (Oxholm) will write about something Bill did or said. And, there are even a few occasions when we will write in the first person, such as "When I saw that . . . " From the context, it will be evident who the "I" is referring to—either Bill or Tom.

We will take the credit and blame for what we say here; however, most of the story is about the many, many great board members, administrators, teachers, parents, and community partners who are all pulling together to provide every student with the highest quality educational experience possible.

We hope you enjoy our story. While *The Wonderful Wizard of Oz* is ultimately an allegory, this story is a true telling. Please join us as we describe for you our journey along the yellow brick road.

NOTE

1. Data have been organized from various Wake County Public School System sources and documents. Please visit the school district's Web site at www.wcpss.net.

Acknowledgments

Writing this book has been fun, but challenging. In the course of our careers, we have written many documents, reports, and articles—but nothing of the nature of this book. We soon recognized that we needed help if we ever hoped to produce the book.

Bill Carruthers (professionally, Dr. William L. Carruthers) was the Senior Director for Grants Administration and Compliance Reporting in the Wake County Public School System. Bill is now retired from the school district. We knew that Bill was an accomplished writer from his success with helping school district personnel secure competitive grant awards, exceeding sixty million dollars. Bill has been an invaluable resource to the two of us—meeting with us evenings and weekends to help keep us moving forward, while helping to edit our writing, synchronize our different writing styles, and clarify our thinking. He has not been hesitant about posing the difficult questions that have challenged our memories, beliefs, values, and assumptions.

We also acknowledge the contributions of significant others in our lives and careers. I, Bill McNeal, wish to personally acknowledge and thank my father, the late William R. McNeal Sr., and my mother, Francis McNeal, for being caring and courageous parents; my wife, Faye, of more than thirty-five years, for being my partner-in-life and advisor; my daughters Tiffany and Crystal, for being my joy; my sons-in-law for making my girls happy, which makes me happy; and the spirit of my recently born grandchildren (twins) for reminding me of what it's all about. I must also acknowledge and thank the Wake County Board of Education members who took a chance on an unlettered son of a minister from Durham, North Carolina. I am thankful for the outstanding teachers, principals, central office staff, and administrative cabinet—all of whom make the Wake County Public School System the success story that it is. I am thankful for the parent, faith, and business community for your unflinching support over the years. And, I am thankful for the students—a wonderful, intellectual, and principled group of young people who made my career in education the joy that it has been. For all of these people and others, I tried to never let you down.

And I, Tom Oxholm, wish to acknowledge and thank my wife, Becky, for her understanding of my passion for education, especially during my service on the board of education and the considerable time this took on top of my regular employment and community service. I thank the owners of Wake Stone Corporation, the Bratton family, for the encouragement they gave me and their support for education. In addition, I am thankful for the support of my brothers, Tobey and Paul, and the spirit of community service we inherited from our mother, and I thank Casper Holroyd, my joyful service mentor and friend. Finally, I will also thank Bill McNeal for all that he taught me and all that his leadership has meant to the students, parents, and educators of Wake County.

Together, we both say thank you to Corwin Press, which provided encouragement every step of the way. We have been fortunate to have had their support.

Ultimately, this book is the story of the many great leaders who, since 1976, have contributed to the success of the Wake County Public School System. We are indebted to you and thank you, everyone!

Corwin Press gratefully acknowledges the contributions of the following individuals:

Robert Bennett
Former Board President
Wyoming Public Schools
Wyoming, MI

Jill M. Gildea
Superintendent
Harrison Elementary School District #36
Wonderlake, IL

Angie Koppang
Associate Professor
University of South Dakota
Vermillion, SD

Elizabeth Lolli, PhD
Superintendent
Monroe Local School District
Monroe, OH

Robert Mayer
Assistant Professor of Educational Administration
University of South Dakota
Vermillion, SD

Janie L. Nusser
Superintendent
South Seneca Central School District
Ovid, NY

Marian White-Hood, PhD
Director of Academics, Principal Support and Accountability
Seeforever & Maya Angelou Public Charter Schools
Washington, DC

About the Authors

Bill McNeal became executive director of the North Carolina Association of School Administrators on July 1, 2006, after retiring from his post as Superintendent of the Wake County Public School System in Raleigh, North Carolina. In his current role, he leads the membership association that serves almost 7,000 public school administrators from all 115 school districts in North Carolina.

Bill is a rarity in public education. He is a "homegrown" superintendent who experienced the entire thirty-year history of the consolidated Wake County Public School System, from the classroom to the boardroom. Aside from his current role and brief stints in the military and teaching in Connecticut, his entire professional career was devoted to Wake County students. In 1974, Bill became a social studies teacher at Carroll Junior High in Wake County. He was promoted to assistant principal at Carroll in 1976, and then served as principal at East Garner Middle and Martin Middle Schools. In 1985, he became an assistant superintendent for administration, then an associate superintendent for auxiliary services, and, in 1992, the associate superintendent for instructional services—an eight-year role as the superintendent's right-hand man responsible for students' academic progress. During this time, he became a key player in the development of the district's Goal 2003. In 2000, the Wake County Board of Education called upon Bill to be superintendent and lead the school system he had served for so many years.

Bill has received many awards and honors for his service to public schools, including being named the National Superintendent of the Year in 2004 by the American Association of School Administrators. In July 2005, he was appointed as the Superintendent Advisor to the North Carolina State Board of Education, a post he held until June 2006. He is a member of a number of boards: WakeMed Foundation; Peace College; Golden Corral; Triangle New School; North Carolina Public School Forum; Education: Everybody's Business Coalition; and Lightner Foundation.

Bill is married to Faye McNeal, a retired guidance counselor, and they have two married daughters, Tiffany Fox (married to Moses) and Crystal Utley (married to Stacy). Recently, Crystal and Stacy gave Bill and Faye their first two grandchildren, twins James Christopher and Tiffany Alexandria. Bill and Faye continue to live in Raleigh, North Carolina.

Tom Oxholm was educated in public and private schools in the suburbs of Philadelphia. He graduated from The University of North Carolina at Chapel Hill in 1976 at age 20 with a degree in business administration, concentration in accounting. He became a CPA in 1979.

Upon graduation he joined the accounting firm KPMG in Raleigh, North Carolina. Since 1986, he has been a Vice President of Wake Stone Corporation in Knightdale, a Raleigh suburb. Wake Stone operates five stone quarries in North and South Carolina. His responsibilities at Wake Stone include finance, accounting, human resources, risk management, and much more for the company and its owners.

His adult life has been one of dedicated public service to the community, primarily in the areas of his church, public education, and health care. Additionally, Tom was a Sunday school leader for teenagers for thirty years. For Wake County's largest hospital system, WakeMed, he serves on the board of directors as finance chair, and has served the WakeMed Foundation in fund- and friend-raising for the last ten years, currently as chairperson. For the last fifteen years, he has been recognized as the area's most influential businessperson in public education. His credentials include Founder of the Wake County Business Education Leadership Council; Friends of Wake County, supporting the 1996, 1999, and 2006 school bonds; and Chair of the School Finance Committee for the Wake Education Partnership, which published the first-ever guide to Wake County Public School System spending—*Show Me the Money*. His recognitions include the 1997 Citizen of the Year for the Town of Knightdale and Wake Education Partnership's 1998 Friend of Education for work with public schools. He also served one four-year term on the Wake County Board of Education. During those four years, he was paid a total of $47,000, all of which he donated to the Wake County Public School System. Tom also serves on the Board of Paragon Commercial Bank in Raleigh, chairing the Audit Committee.

Tom is an avid, low-handicap golfer. He and Becky, his wife of twenty-five years, greatly enjoy their four grown children: Katherine, Birk, Patrick, and Eleanor.

Leadership in Context

We know that educational leaders come in many shapes and sizes and that leadership takes many forms. We also know that different styles of leadership are more suitable at different times or in different situations. While the interaction between an individual's personal style and the context in which the leadership plays out may vary, it is our premise that there are some essential characteristics of leadership that apply to any individual or situation. Two such characteristics that we believe apply to leaders in public education are the individual's value system and the individual's use of business practices. To best appreciate our story of the Wake County Public School System, the values we believe educational leaders should manifest, and the utility of business practices in public education, it is helpful to have an understanding of the thirty-year historical context of the Wake County Public School System.[1]

Located in Wake County, North Carolina, with Raleigh, the state capital, its major municipality, the Wake County Public School System was created in 1976 from a merger of the Raleigh City Schools and the Wake County Schools.[2] At that time, Raleigh City Schools was 38 percent minority and the Wake County Schools was 23 percent minority. The Raleigh City Schools was threatened with loss of federal funds due to a finding by the U.S. Office of Civil Rights (OCR) that the Raleigh City Schools had violated Title VI of the Civil Rights Act of 1963.

Following merger, the merged school district was required to submit a plan to OCR to remedy the Title VI violations found by OCR. The board of education of this newly formed, countywide school district made a commitment to provide for a desegregated education for all students. The district resolved to establish and maintain a racial balance of 15–45 percent minority enrollment in each school. This ratio reflected a 15 percent variance from what was at that time the average of 30 percent minority population across all schools.

The plan accomplished desegregation of the Wake County Public School System by redrawing boundaries of the schools, taking into account a number of factors, including the racial composition of the communities, where schools were located, and transportation patterns. As a result of the successful implementation of the desegregation plan, the county was able to resolve the student assignment issues with OCR, and in 1979, the district was declared a unitary school district by the United States District Court.

During the period of the merger, the business community was a strong advocate in favor of merger. While OCR may have provided the impetus for merger, once the notion was entertained, the business community appreciated the economics of merger, including stemming white flight from the inner city schools, keeping all schools fully enrolled, and providing an equitable and quality education for all students. Now, with the perspective of thirty years' history, it is apparent how important this courageous decision to merge has been to Wake County's thriving economy. Throughout the thirty-year history, there have been many decisions of similar import that have contributed to sustaining and enhancing this vitality.

In 1982, the district's mandatory student assignment plan was supplemented by a voluntary "Schools of Choice" magnet school plan. Prior to 1982, the school district had established a couple of magnet schools, but this number was dramatically increased in the Schools of Choice plan. In the 1982–83 school year, the Schools of Choice plan designated twenty-eight of the district's schools magnet schools, with these elementary, middle, and high schools implementing a variety of magnet themes. Each magnet school was assigned a base neighborhood population and also recruited students from other areas of the county. Students not in the base population applied to enroll at a magnet school and a lottery was used to select students; at that time, race of the student was one consideration used in the lottery selection process.

With enrollment growing year after year, in the 1987–88 year, the chairperson of the county commissioners and the county manager suggested to school district leaders that they investigate year-round schooling with the notion being that a multitrack, year-round school could enroll more students than one operating on a traditional calendar. Following a couple years of study, a year-round school was opened as a newly built school in the 1989–90 school year—the first in North Carolina and first magnet year-round in the nation. In subsequent years, more year-round schools have been established, typically schools that are newly built and opened as year-rounds. However, with enrollment growth continuing and school seats becoming increasingly difficult to find, the building of new schools was unable to keep up with the growth; the school board then voted to convert twenty-two existing elementary and middle schools to a multitrack year-round calendar starting with the 2007–08 year. Following these conversions, in 2007–08, the school district operated forty-six year-round schools (thirty-eight elementary schools with Grades K–5, and eight middle schools with Grades 6–8). At the time this book went to press, there was a court ruling that parents must give their consent for children to attend a year-round school.[3]

As previously indicated, the Wake County Public School System (WCPSS) had used race of the student as one of the factors considered in student assignment. However, by 1999, there were concerns among school district leaders that the use of race in this manner was being interpreted as illegal by the federal courts. WCPSS had never been under a court-ordered desegregation plan; however, leery of how the courts were now viewing race-based assignment plans, WCPSS school board members voted to remove race as a factor in the district's magnet schools' lottery. In subsequent discussions, the school board developed and implemented in the 1999–2000 year a student assignment plan they believed to be more instructionally sound, based on the variables of family income and student achievement. Under this plan, the school board sought to maintain diversity across all its schools with targets of no school having more than 40 percent of its students receiving free or reduced-price lunch or more than 25 percent performing below grade level. For a more detailed discussion of the school district's efforts to maintain diverse and healthy schools, an article by Todd Silberman, a reporter with the *News and Observer*, is suggested reading.[4]

For most of the school district's history, there has been ceaseless growth in student enrollment. For example, in 1981–82, the year prior to the Schools of Choice plan, the student enrollment in the district was 52,000. Now, in the 2007–08 school year, the student enrollment is more than 134,000. There are administrators and teachers who have taught in the school district this entire time and have seen it grow from a relatively bucolic school district to one that is now the nineteenth largest in the nation. And, the district's growth continues without letup in the twenty-first century. In the next three years, it is projected that the district will open another fifteen schools. Since the merger, every WCPSS superintendent has had to contend with growth as indicated in Figure 1.1.

Figure 1.1   WCPSS Enrollment Growth[5]

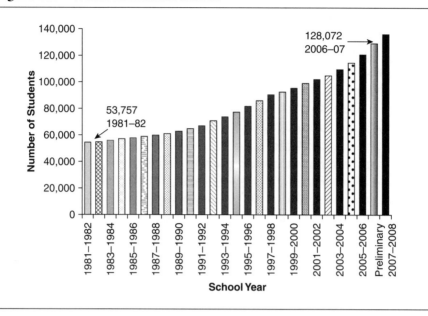

Unquestionably, this growth has impacted administrative and instructional processes in the district, and we believe a case can be made that the growth has made us stronger. Just to keep up with growth, we have had to become better at what we do—how we build buildings, how we instruct students, and how we develop leaders. We have had to become better at the business of education.

While many school districts in the nation will not be facing issues associated with growth, the business principles and practices that we describe in this book remain relevant for all leaders. Even in static situations or school districts experiencing declining enrollment, there is no substitute for challenging all school leaders to be the best at what they do, and this includes the superintendent.

Having the advantage of working in the school district since 1974, Bill has worked for all of the previous five superintendents and he has had the opportunity to see the office of the superintendency from a relatively close perspective. Until his retirement June 30, 2006, Bill was a Wake County school district employee for every day of the school district's existence. From Bill's perspective, each of his predecessors made significant contributions to the school district's success.

Following a national search conducted by the school board of the newly merged school district, the era of Dr. John Murphy's tenure (1976–1981) as the first superintendent of the school district was marked chiefly with an emphasis on implementing the unified administration of the school district. The transition from two school districts—one chiefly urban and one chiefly rural—to a single district was not without bumps and bruises and heartaches, but it was accomplished with relative efficiency. By 1980, new employees being hired into the unified district saw few if any vestiges of the old city and county school districts.

Again conducting a national search, the board of education next hired Dr. Walter Marks (1981–1984), whose leadership was instrumental in implementing the district's Schools of Choice plan establishing magnet schools to promote diversity in school enrollment. With many downtown schools under-enrolled, in disrepair, and in jeopardy of closure, the district was able to reinvent these schools as magnets, renovate them, and fill them to capacity. Since implementing the Schools of Choice plan, no downtown school has been closed and the district has conducted many school renovations to maintain the adequacy of facilities at all schools. Although the magnet program became a bright star for the school system, there were questions that developed over whether the cost of the magnet program was being correctly reported, and Dr. Marks resigned in 1984.

Subsequently, Dr. Robert Bridges was hired to be the district's third superintendent (1984–1988). Dr. Bridges was an internal candidate for the position and had worked his whole career in Wake County. Before being hired as superintendent, Bridges had been the deputy superintendent for the school district. Following the controversy over the magnet schools program on the heels of Dr. Marks's resignation, Dr. Bridges was seen as a steady hand and calming influence. Dr. Bridges worked to raise the productivity level of all employees through business practices, including empowering employees to take more ownership and to be more accountable to the community.

Following the leadership of Murphy, Marks, and Bridges, the school district was now well established with its feet solidly on the ground. We knew who we were, what we valued, and where we wanted to go. Dr. Bridges then retired and the district again conducted a national search for a superintendent, hiring Dr. Robert Wentz in July 1989. While the district had been growing in enrollment for the entire decade, this growth was beginning to accelerate and the board's search had led them to Dr. Wentz, who came from Clark County, Nevada, where the school district had been experiencing significant growth. Wentz's tenure (1989–1993) with WCPSS was marked with efforts to manage this growth, for instance, through the expansion of year-round schools along with the continuing development of magnet schools.

It is interesting to point out that this period of time, the 1990s, is when information technologies and the Internet first began to make significant inroads into the public's consciousness. In a short time, school districts everywhere would be challenged to keep abreast of the latest developments, chief of which is communicating with stakeholders—staff, students, parents, and the broader community. From this point forward, superintendents and school leaders in general would realize how necessary it is to become better at the business of communication—to get the school district's message out before the public by all means possible—if only to stay ahead of everyone else who will be talking about you on the Internet!

Upon Dr. Wentz's departure, Bill McNeal briefly served as an interim superintendent for the school district from December 1995 to June 1996, after which Dr. Jim Surratt, formally superintendent of Plano, Texas, was hired following a national search. The board recruited Dr. Surratt because of his record of creativity, forward-thinking nature, and focus on technology. During Dr. Surratt's tenure, the school district formulated a districtwide technology plan that standardized computer use across the district, another standard of business practice. Interestingly, during Surratt's tenure, the one bond issue to not be supported by the public was said to have failed in part due to the amount of money that was in the bond request for new technology. Dr. Surratt resigned soon thereafter and Bill McNeal was named the school district's sixth superintendent beginning July 2000; he retired in June 2006.

As authors of this book, we leave the legacy of our tenure for others to judge; however, we both agree that whatever we were able to accomplish was because of the leadership and accomplishments of our predecessors, superintendents and board members, and that of all the WCPSS employees, administrators, faculty, staff, parents, and wonderful students.

We will close this history with a recent quote from North Carolina State Senator Vernon Malone who was Chairperson of the Wake County Board of Education at the time of the merger in 1976:

> Merging the Raleigh and Wake County school systems was not an easy thing to do, but it was the right thing to do. We worked to create a school system that would serve as a foundation for a proud unified community, and we succeeded. The community should be extremely proud that we were able to integrate and merge the school system in an uncomfortable climate and we never lost a single day of school because of violence. Many have devoted their careers and their lives to helping this system succeed. Much has been accomplished and there is more yet to do. My hope is that the efforts of the past will light the path for those who are building the next 30 years of Wake County Public School System's legacy now and into the future.[6]

This is our hope as well.

NOTES

1. Much of history is storytelling from the perspective of those who have lived the history. At the Wake County Public School System's Web site, there is a collection of these stories and other information that provide insights into the personalities and events since 1976; please visit http://www.wcpss.net/history/index.html.

2. The story of this merger and the courage required of school officials, elected officials, businesses, and community leaders to see the merger through is told in *A Community United: Celebrating 30 Years of Courageous Leadership*, published by the Wake Education Partnership, Raleigh, NC, and retrieved October 27, 2007, from http://wakeedpartnership.org/publications/d/WCPSS-30th.pdf.

3. At the time of publication, the school district is appealing the court ruling, and Judge Howard Manning's ruling on this issue can be found at http://ads.news14char lotte.com/Wake_Schools_Ruling.pdf, retrieved October 27, 2007.

4. Silberman, T. (n.d.). *Wake County Schools: A question of balance.* Retrieved October 27, 2007, from http://www.tcf.org/Publications/Education/silberman.pdf.

5. Wake County Public School System. (2007). *Demographics.* Retrieved October 20, 2007, from www.wcpss.net/demographics/.

6. Wake Education Partnership. (2006). *A Community United: Celebrating 30 Years of Courageous Leadership.* Raleigh, NC: Author. Retrieved October 27, 2007, from www.wakeedpartnership.org/publications/d/WCPSS-30th.pdf.

2

Leadership and Courage

Why, Zeke! You're just as scared as I am!

—Dorothy in *The Wizard of Oz*

The Cowardly Lion is an apt icon for courage. Before this leonine character emerges in Dorothy's bizarre fantasy, we meet his real character, Zeke, a field hand of her Auntie Em and Uncle Henry, when Zeke rescues Dorothy from the pig pen after she has fallen in among the pigs. Both Dorothy and Hickory (who will later manifest in Dorothy's fantasy as the Tin Woodman) remark on how white and frightened Zeke appears after performing his heroic feat. Zeke is frightened, yet he performs heroically—exposing himself to danger to save Dorothy. Not only do fictional heroes need courage, but the rest of us in real life must also muster it to do the dangerous or unpopular thing, whether it is a teenager turning down drugs despite his friends' insistence that it is the "cool" thing to do, or a school superintendent who puts the needs of children first despite what is popular or politically expedient.

There are many forms of courage. The soldier evidences courage. The patient struggling with cancer evidences courage. The mother giving birth to her first child evidences courage. The leader not giving in to political pressure evidences courage. And, educators determined to make a difference for every child evidence courage every day. Being accountable for producing positive results is a form of courage. Setting high goals for positive results is a form of courage. Standing up to public school detractors takes courage. Seeking innovative perspectives on teaching takes courage. Subjecting your work to an independent evaluation takes courage. We will discuss these and other forms of courage in this chapter.

In the field of education, leaders who exhibit courage will find that it can be a lonely position that can make them unpopular. If popularity is what you seek, then select some other occupation. The serious business of schooling requires leaders who know right from wrong and choose to do right. The leader who brings stakeholders to the tables, including detractors, to seek their opinion on key decisions is to be commended. That, in our opinion, is a high form of leadership because it guarantees that information will be shared, and it also builds bridges that form the basis of a personal relationship and respect. Ultimately, it is the respect of your supporters and detractors that will pay huge dividends for your organization.

The number one reason for leading courageously in the storm is the message it sends to the young people who look to us for guidance; clearly the message is that courageous decisions are worth the sacrifice because they form the basis of our integrity and respect. The courage to merge a school district in the mid-1970s, as happened in Wake County, or to determine that no school will be disproportionate with its number of poor children, reflected in the school district's student assignment plan, is an example of leadership in the storm. Show us that kind of courage and we will show you a place where children excel.

ACCOUNTABILITY

Accountability. Business people love the word. Educators traditionally hate it. It doesn't need to be that way.

Employees in modern business practice are held accountable. Performance criteria and evaluations are the norm. Being fired for not getting the job done happens all the time. Lack of resources? An empty excuse. Too late? Too bad. Do better next year? Not here. Business people know, at any given time, for what they will be held accountable and what the rewards and penalties are likely to be. Business leaders know that accountability causes employees—from the CEO down—to focus their energy on what is important. The emphasis on accountability produces results—usually the results leaders are seeking.[1] Public school educators, on the other hand, would rather not deal with the issue of accountability and historically have not. They are so used to taking abuse from the public that they typically are unwilling to engage in internal criticism, especially written.

Prior to Bill McNeal's superintendency, Wake County's superintendents rarely received comprehensive written evaluations, and there were few prior agreed-upon performance criteria or ways to measure results stemming from the superintendent's leadership. Wake County Board of Education members did not want something in writing that could not be defended if some disagreement with the superintendent arose, and some superintendents were similarly comfortable with the absence of written performance measures. Consequently, very few comprehensive evaluations were done on the superintendent's job performance.

Other factors in education have steered administrators and teachers away from accountability. For one, few are rewarded for doing a great job, except for the pride individuals could take in knowing that they made a difference in a child's life. For another, most teachers have tenure or union contracts that provide protection no matter how well or how poorly they perform. With job security, who wants to be bothered with accountability? And, with guaranteed annual salary increases (either by contract or legislation) that are the same for everyone, there have been few incentives to excel, to take a risk, to stand out from the crowd. In situations like these, accountability could serve no purpose but finger-pointing. So what can be done? Answers must be sought at the state, school district, and school building levels.

In North Carolina, the ABCs (Accountability, Basics, Control) of Public Education program was developed by the State Board of Education in response to the 1995 General Assembly. This plan established guidelines and target goals for annual progress for each school relative to the test results of the year before. Teachers at a school could earn bonuses if the students at the school achieved those goals. The ABCs program has created an incentive that has worked well on a school-by-school basis in a state where teachers have traditionally been underpaid. With the ABCs program, the state introduced a measure of accountability at the school level—schools were "graded," so to speak, in terms of whether the school met achievement standards and teachers were financially rewarded if the school met these standards. Subsequently, the Wake County Public School System (WCPSS) took this emphasis on accountability to a higher level in a step that took considerable courage on the part of board members and administrators.

Like most school districts, WCPSS has a mission statement but, unlike many districts, WCPSS holds itself accountable to measure up to this mission. The mission of the Wake County Public School System reads as follows: *The Wake County Public School System will educate each student to be a responsible and productive citizen who can effectively manage future challenges.* To be held accountable for achieving this mission, WCPSS wanted to provide some level of assurance to the community that it was willing to take this mission seriously and achieve higher academic standards for its students. WCPSS recognized that it needed to establish a metric by which the community could tell what progress the school district was making toward fulfilling its mission. Setting this metric—a stretch goal—led to some extraordinarily positive results.

Setting Stretch Goals

Developing the lofty mission of the school system, in turn, led to a process that involved the community in the formulation of a stretch goal.[2] The school district collected input about a stretch goal from the business sector, parent groups, teacher organizations, and the division of principals and assistant principals, among numerous other groups. The process of collecting this input literally had the effect of rallying the village around the school system. Could we identify a goal that would satisfy all of these interest groups? What single, overarching goal would these diverse groups all recognize as one that would reflect our purpose in public education, be meaningful to all citizens, and set a lofty standard for achievement?

In the summer of 1998, following a community education summit, the Wake County Board of Education held two retreats to tackle this issue. It was then that the board of education established Goal 2003, stating: *By 2003, 95 percent of students tested in Grades 3 and 8 will be at or above grade level as measured by the North Carolina End-of-Grade (EOG) tests.* This goal didn't say the district wanted 95 percent of just white students or Asian students at or above grade level; it stated 95 percent of *all* students (white, Asian, Latino/Hispanic, African American, Native American, free and reduced-price lunch students, academically gifted, etc.—*all* students). Although the goal was written for third- and eighth-grade students, we knew that all grade levels would be impacted over the course of the five years set for achieving the goal. Third-grade teachers would want the K–2 teachers to ready their students for the third grade, and the eighth-grade teachers would want the same of the earlier grade level teachers. High school teachers might feel as if the goal did not apply to them, but they would surely want the district to achieve success, better preparing students for high school.

It is important to note that we had settled on a single goal. Whereas many school districts will create a lengthy collection of goals, trying to address a great variety of desired outcomes, we had identified one easy-to-remember goal that represented the sum of everything we hoped to accomplish with students. It is also important to note that no additional funding was associated with this goal. We were idealistic and optimistic; we intended to achieve the goal with available resources.

For many in our community, the goal seemed absurd. For some population groups and regions of the county, with percentages in the sixties and seventies, this goal might appear quite unrealistic. We heard from many who questioned this goal. With so much ground to cover, such a goal was surely unachievable and, if it was unachievable, why set the district up for failure and community ridicule? This was 1998; how could such progress be made by 2003, in only five years? Why not set a more realistic goal? How about 85 percent or 90 percent? While many questioned the goal on these premises, we also heard from many who found the goal to be exciting. The notion that we would raise achievement for all students in the entire district was the kind of challenge that many in our county enthusiastically endorsed.

We knew that some dramatic work needed to be done if all students were to make this mark. Our majority white students were not performing at the 95 percent level, and our minority students—in particular African American and Latino/Hispanic—were performing well below this level. Factor in other population groups such as students with disabilities, free and reduced-price lunch students, and students whose first language was not English, and you can easily see this was a daunting task. Was this foolish or was this courage? We didn't know the answer, but school leaders mustered the courage to commit to this standard of accountability and we did so very publicly, committing to this goal in the belief that it should be done and faith that it could be done. Would the Cowardly Lion in *The Wizard of Oz* have done anything different? Maybe it requires the courage of a lion to take such a step—simply because it was the right step.

For us, the right decision was made. The simplicity of this one goal was that it didn't single out a particular group, but required that 95 percent be the goal for all. In times past, when a group was singled out, this often resulted in the "blame game," which usually worked counter to the objective. Even though there was a general understanding that African American and Latino/Hispanic children lagged the furthest in test results, this was often not discussed in open forums. The unwritten rule was to not point our fingers at any particular group. Should someone dare to do so, even with the best of intentions, that person could risk being considered racist. However, Goal 2003 changed all of that thinking by forcing this very discussion, requiring the school district and community to recognize differences and step up to the challenges of improving education for all students.

The goal energized all facets of our community with its single focus. Each group could see its worth and the impact it would have on their children. African American and Latino/Hispanic families could see a commitment to improve the academic standing of their children and at the same time white and Asian families could be sure their children's needs would be addressed as well. The tightrope we walked was trying to close the achievement gap while ensuring that advanced students also grew academically. Resources could not be taken from the best performing students to help the lower performing students—we knew that parents of gifted children would protest, and rightfully so. Any perception that we weren't serving our best and brightest students was aggressively countered, knowing that such a perception could result in the defection of these students to private, parochial, charter, or home schools. In adopting Goal 2003, the district could end up damaging itself if it led to parents leaving public education.

We knew we had gone out on a limb. Would a business ever announce a new product, new service, or higher level of product or service without having spent huge amounts of resources to be sure it was achievable? Probably not, but nor had we. We knew our students *were* capable. Would a business ever announce any new product line until they were close to success? Probably not, but nor had we. We knew we were striving for excellence and were confident that we had the courage, brains, and heart necessary to be successful. And what has been our success?

One measure of the success we achieved in pursuit of Goal 2003 was in securing new resources and making better use of existing resources. Surely, this is a measure of success that any business would admire. While Goal 2003 was set with the knowledge that additional resources were not guaranteed, over time the goal became a mantra for organizing the resources needed to support the goal. The Wake County Board of County Commissioners appropriated some additional funds to support the goal,[3] and school administrators reviewed all budget items to identify funds to support this goal. Through the effort of the commissioners and realignment of existing school district resources, we were able to cover a portion of the new and expanded strategies that we began rolling out in pursuit of the goal, without major tax increases.

Most significantly, our success is evident in the achievement gains our students made. Figure 2.1 depicts the composite percentage of our students in third through eighth grade who passed both of North Carolina's reading and mathematics End-of-Grade exams for the years 1994–2003, the latter year being the point in time when we planned to have achieved the 95 percent goal. We didn't completely achieve our goal, but our progress was still very remarkable. While it is not possible to attribute a statistical cause-and-effect relationship between establishing the goal in 1998 and the rising achievement gains in subsequent years, still, it is interesting to note how Figure 2.1 shows that the year 1998 is when achievement gains began to show a marked and steady increase each subsequent year.

Figure 2.1   Percentage of Third- Through Eighth-Grade Students Passing Both Reading and Math State Exams[4]

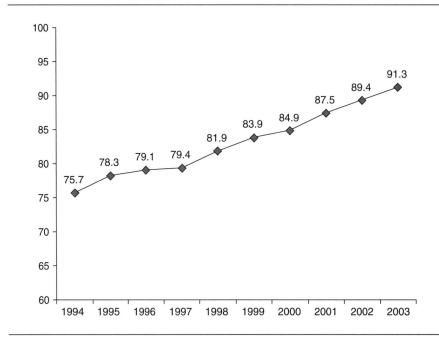

In Figure 2.2, we provide another look at the achievement gains students made in the years between 1994 and 2003, showing that each of our major racial population groups made steady gains over the years. The achievement gap that existed in 1994 between the highest and lowest performing groups, almost 40 percentage points, had narrowed to less than 20 percentage points by 2003. It is especially impressive that all population groups made steady gains—the highest performing population groups as well as the lowest performing population groups.

All students made gains and the persistent and debilitating achievement gap (impacting students and staff alike) had been significantly narrowed. The school district had shown what can happen when men and women of courage choose to put themselves to the test and elevate expectations for all students. This was not easy for teachers, administrators, students, or parents. We are talking about hard work, dedication, and being constantly on guard for negativism, an attitude that was often abetted by the ever-present enemies of public education. However, we would not be deterred; we knew we were on the right path. Setting Goal 2003—a stretch goal—was courageous.

Figure 2.2   Closing the Achievement Gap

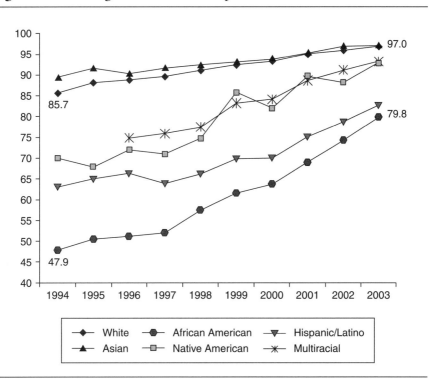

Responding to Detractors

While Goal 2003 addressed accountability for achievement results, a more commonly understood form of accountability is fiscal management. When you're dealing with fiscal accountability and other people's money, you can bet that you will have your share of critics and detractors. The best way to respond to detractors is to open the doors and let them in the house. That takes courage!

One of the more common fiscal criticisms is that the school district is a bloated bureaucracy. We are criticized for not spending the public's money wisely, for giving students too much homework, for not considering family vacation plans when we set the next year's calendar, for X, for Y, and for Z. Any criticism you have heard, we have heard as well.

It is safe to say that public schools have become so accustomed to criticism that the path often chosen for dealing with critics is to slam the information door in their faces. All too frequently, critics are ignored.

This behavior may come from a mistaken belief that even if detractors had all the facts, they would not deal with them forthrightly, but would skew the information to meet their own preconceptions. However, we believe that many of the outspoken critics of public education often have very limited information. If our premise is correct, then we should respond to our detractors by educating them. After all, we're in the "business" of education! We maintain that all information not of a proprietary or confidential nature needs to be available to the public for scrutiny and readily accessible on the school district's Web site (www.wcpss.net). Moreover, when more information is required, we gladly supply it. Businesses refer to this as transparency.

Following the financial debacles of Enron and WorldCom in the early part of the new century, businesses began to adopt the practice of making their records more open to the public eye. Of course, Congress mandated it for all publicly held companies. Now, all companies share information with their employees, customers, and investors in their effort to be best.[5]

This approach requires courage, and if handled improperly, can be costly to a school district. We appreciate that some of this information could in turn be used by our critics to add fuel to their fire, but it has been our general experience that our critics instead become more enlightened. We can see this enlightenment develop as the tenor of their argument with us begins to change. Additionally, the debate helps to also inform those who are sitting on the sidelines. These individuals—the silent majority—become more educated because of the increased flow of information to the public via the media.

With our budget, we decided that an open-book approach was the right thing to do, even though this would probably mean more work for our staff. We felt strongly that what the school district was doing was right, proper, and defensible; we also felt that through making even more information available to the public, citizens with an interest in public education might well come up with ideas to improve what the district was doing. If so, the district would move to implement these ideas. Businesses do this all the time with focus groups. Using small, controlled groups to determine the public's interest and/or perspective is just good business sense. However, most school districts do not have the financial wherewithal to conduct varied focus groups, so we made our whole community a focus group. Taking such a stance could be heresy to many educators. Imagine, educators listening to noneducators telling us what to do!

I'm sure our critics were surprised by our reaction. Instead of slamming the door in their faces, we were inviting them to come in, take a seat at the table, and share their ideas—which we took seriously. From the standpoint of credibility, this stance is critical.

We have seen school districts give voice to this approach, but too often only on paper. Many school boards have appointed task forces and oversight committees. But, the school boards controlled who served and controlled the results. Furthermore, members of these task forces and committees often colluded in this process. By virtue of being friends of, or advocates for, the school district, there were no fears of what recommendations would be forthcoming. It was a totally controlled environment among friends. Unfortunately, this approach is all too transparent to the serious critics of the school district, and the committees become another target of these critics. Additionally, the media will note who the committee members are and question the credibility of the process. No credibility equals no accountability. These committees may be comfortable for educators, but they do little to silence our critics, or—just possibly— identify a new and innovative approach to addressing the criticisms. Imagine the loss if we miss an opportunity to improve our systems because of not listening well to serious criticism.

Opening our books was the approach school district administrators took with the County Commissioner's Task Force on Public Spending, including task force members who we knew were determined critics of our public schools. Subsequently, having had this opportunity to freely inspect the books, the Task Force recommended no cuts in public school spending. Since that time, two Citizen Advisory Committees were formed in the county and they too conducted in-depth reviews of school district spending (1999–2000 on capital spending and 2001–03 on operational spending). The approach taken by WCPSS was the same—give them what they ask for and do so promptly.

The 1999 Citizen Advisory Committee (CAC) came about as a result of the school district's first and only failed bond issue. Since 1980, Wake County had been going to its taxpayers for hundreds of millions of dollars to construct new schools and renovate old ones, just to keep up with tremendous growth in student population.[6] For a number of reasons, the bond issue was defeated in June 1999 by a *two to one margin*. Our critics came out in force and won the day—or so they thought. Without the bond, we would struggle in the years to come to build the needed new schools and maintain the existing schools. But then, that wasn't a concern of the critics.

With boards of education in North Carolina unable to levy taxes, the responsibility for providing school buildings and seats for students rests largely with the county commissioners. In the summer of 1999, our commissioners wisely commissioned a CAC task force to analyze what went wrong with the bond issue. The task force agreed on a chairman, a recently retired CPA from a large national firm, and both boards (school and county) jointly appointed a forty-person committee of school supporters and critics. As reported by the news media, this task force had credibility. One year later, that committee submitted its list of twenty-nine recommendations for changes in the way the school system and county provided and cared for school buildings. All but two of the recommendations were implemented right away. The other two (lifting the state's cap on charter schools and creating a school construction authority) were studied but could not be accomplished without further study and legislative action.

Our community was satisfied that the task force had performed its job well, and in the next year approved the largest bond issue to that point in time. The school district's willingness to include detractors of the school system in the CAC process, an open-book approach, and commitment to live with the recommendations of the CAC were relatively novel ideas at the time and led the school district to better ways of doing business, as well as increased public confidence in the school system.

The second CAC was organized upon the request of the county commissioners to decide whether school district administrative monies were being spent wisely and whether the district needed more or less money from the county to be successful. This time, a smaller committee jointly appointed by the commissioners and school district, and with resources for consultants, took two years to reach their conclusions. The open-book approach was used again and the conclusions were overwhelmingly in favor of increased funding for schools. In 2006–07, the county commissioners again called for a CAC to review capital spending practices in the district. After a year of study, this latest CAC recommended for commissioners a variety of possible ways to reduce programs and save money. Surely, there will be more CACs in the future.

We will end this piece by paraphrasing Mahatma Gandhi's response to being attacked, "First [your detractors] ignore you; then they laugh at you; then they fight you; then you win." For us, being attacked by our detractors only provides more opportunities to inform and educate them, to gain even greater public support in the process, and to possibly identify new and better solutions.

Annual Independent Audits by the Community

One of the constant challenges in public education is to prove that money is being spent wisely so that if more tax dollars are needed, the public will have confidence that the money is truly necessary. The public generally understands the great importance of public education with respect to economic development and the future of their community and country. But, if they feel that money is being spent wastefully, they will withdraw support for the school system.

We have learned over the years how difficult it is to educate a public when large sums of their money are being spent. In 1998, the Wake Education Partnership (WEP) decided that the public had little under-standing of public education spending.[7] The operating budget for 1997–98 was nearly half a billion dollars! It did not matter how many students there were, critics could easily complain about the total tax dollars being spent, simply due to the size of our school district. WEP decided that a little education would help improve the community's appreciation of public education.

It is not easy to explain how $500 million is spent to an audience of people who do not have hours to devote to learning the material. On our part and that of WEP, hundreds of hours were spent in developing a twelve-page presentation for the public. Five community forums were held to explain the handouts but less than 300 people attended—in a commu-nity of over 600,000 at the time. Finally, a glossy, easy-to-read booklet was printed and distributed through public speaking engagements and in the local newspaper; however, 140,000 copies later most people were still in the dark about the budget. Getting people to learn the details of a half-billion dollar budget was proving to be a challenge.

Consequently, with the cooperation of the school system, beginning in 2000, WEP agreed to sponsor an independent annual audit of the school district's spending. This was not an audit like the kind produced by certified public accountants. This was an audit by the community to determine if the community felt it was getting a good return on their tax dollar invest-ment. There was a commitment to do this for at least four years, with a goal to improve the district's credibility—and *accountability*—through the process of collecting, interpreting, and reporting to the community.

Generally speaking, school systems would rather not participate in this kind of event—putting themselves on the line, year after year, to public scrutiny and criticism. But, here too, the school system showed courage. We pledged our commitment of time and information without any control over what would be produced in the report, or what the conclusions would be. The district's willingness to participate in this joint effort has paid divi-dends many times over. Because of the involvement of so many people in the process, these people have become supporters of the system with many of them going on to become outspoken leaders in the community.

Due in part to these annual audits, we believe the district's credibility and accountability are improving. The level of understanding and general acceptance of the fact that a large school district will spend a lot of money, and can do it wisely, has become more commonplace in the community.

While the WEP reports have noted various criticisms and concerns about the school district, in these reports the school district compares very favorably with other systems in North Carolina and well-known ones outside the state. We hope that WEP continues this project as long as there is the need to educate citizens about public education.

Winning the public's support is not a one-time event; it is continuous and must take place on several levels. Submitting oneself to public scrutiny takes a lot of courage. Along with improving credibility and accountability, through this scrutiny we are realizing an additional benefit. The benefit is an increase in the self-confidence that our administrators and school board members feel. We know that they have received good reports for years, and we have no fear of responding to a request for information. We believe in our school system. In time, this self-confidence infects all school employees. Being confident, being proud of who we are, and the work we do helps us accept the challenges of this work.

Below are some ideas for your consideration, whether you are a large or small school district.

WHAT YOU CAN DO TO IMPROVE

- Embrace accountability and transparency
- Set a stretch goal
- Open the doors and books to critics
- Make information easy to get for the public
- Use your community as a focus group
- Invite citizen advisory committees to examine your spending practices and make recommendations for improvement
- Encourage citizen groups to "audit" what you do and compare to other school districts
- Seek to continuously improve accountability and spending practices

LEADERSHIP

Every business and every school district will have a leader at its helm or, in a few instances, there may be co-leaders. How an organization selects the right leader for the purpose at hand may be the single most important decision a business or a school district will make. Selecting this leader will set the organization on a particular course of action for at least a couple of years, will redefine the organization's culture as each leader brings his or her leadership style to the role, and will have significant fiscal implications for the organization in the coming years. And, because leadership does not occur in a vacuum, how the organization evaluates its leadership will also be an important decision. There are tried-and-true methods for making these decisions and they generally work well; however, sometimes, it is necessary to step outside the box when making these decisions; sometimes it is necessary to be creative in the selection and evaluation of a leader.

Selecting a Superintendent

The most important duty for an elected board of education is the selection and supervision of the superintendent. For superintendents, there is a parallel in that their most important decision is the selection of school principals. And, in business, there is a parallel with the selection of the CEO. Ask any business board of directors and they will unanimously tell you that selecting the right CEO for their business and appropriately supervising him or her is their main task. Ask CEOs and they in turn will tell you that their most important responsibility is hiring good staff. While education and business both recognize the importance of these hiring decisions, the two groups typically approach these decisions differently.

In the business setting, the board of directors makes sure that a succession plan is in place should the CEO suddenly die, become disabled, or depart for greener pastures.[8] The CEO often has performance criteria that include the adequate preparation of the next in line for the job. Having a successor ready has numerous benefits, as one can imagine. There is no delay for a selection process, no learning curve for the new person, no shifting of agendas, no waiting for a new vision, no unnecessary sudden changes in corporate direction. When a qualified successor is not readily available, this can exact a toll on the progress of the organization.

School systems, especially large school systems with their elected boards, often approach succession planning quite differently. If we ask why this is the case, we can identify a variety of reasons. In a school system, the board make-up is not usually experienced businesspeople, the membership of the board changes with every election (two to four years), politics often enter into the selection process, sitting superintendents may view prepared successors as threats, the bureaucracy reinforces protecting one's turf, and so forth. Despite reasons such as these, we maintain that the selection process should not be any different in school systems than it is in business. Let's take Wake County as an example.

From the point when the city and county school systems merged in 1976, there have been seven superintendents, including Bill McNeal. (Following Bill's retirement in 2006, Dr. Del Burns was named as the seventh superintendent.) In 1976, the very first superintendent was selected by the newly combined city and county boards from among the top administrators interviewed internally and externally.

For the next twenty years, with the exception of Dr. Bob Bridges's tenure, each time there was a turnover in the superintendency, the elected boards each adopted what they believed was the best approach to selecting the new superintendent—they conducted national searches. Each board identified competencies relevant to the needs of the school district at the time (e.g., introducing magnet schools, establishing year-round schools, managing an emerging large school district). And, each board identified hiring criteria that they believed were important (e.g., years of experience as a superintendent, holding a doctorate degree).

In WCPSS, following each national search, each board ended up with what you would expect—finalists for the job who looked great on paper, had great references, and interviewed well. However, whether they would fit in with the school district and community, and also be good leaders of our principals and teachers, was unknown. Basically, when a national search is conducted, a great deal about the new superintendent remains unknown. Further adding to these unknowns, the newly selected superintendent may choose to bring administrators from the previous school district. Generally, the school system gets a superintendent who might make it three to five years before wearing out his or her welcome.

During those three to five years, coming from outside the school district, this superintendent will necessarily spend a year or two trying to gain the confidence of the top administrators and principals, a year or two trying to implement the changes, and the last year looking for the next job and higher pay. Around the country this is a very common scenario. In large urban districts, a superintendency is seen to be a three- to five-year job at best, and most systems just hope they get someone who will keep the ship sailing, maybe not any faster or better, but at least remaining afloat.

In January 2000, after four and one half years on the job, the WCPSS superintendent at the time announced he was leaving. His departure followed on the heels of a school bond that the community voted down the previous June, and certainly he had been looking for several months for the next job. At the time, the nine-member board of education was in transition. The board had four new members just a few months into their terms and four whose range of experience was six to fifteen years. As had been the norm in the district, the experienced board chair announced that the district would retain a search firm to assist in a national search. Although we were then a 100,000-student system with several very experienced administrators in the district, the idea of not doing a national search was rejected out of hand.

In a national search, the tendency to group think is difficult to resist. Typically, a national search begins by seeking the community's involvement. Without question, community involvement must be a part of the search process, but when the starting point for the search is the entire nation, the group members tend to rely on so-called tried-and-true criteria such as previous experience as a superintendent or that proverbial seal of purported excellence—the doctorate. Like water running downhill following the path of least resistance, there are few who are likely to question such seemingly fundamental criteria. Unfortunately, some very excellent candidates can be discouraged from applying or overlooked in the process of a national search—especially the in-house candidate. Yes, experience as a superintendent can be valuable and the doctorate's degree might be indicative of a particular set of skills and competencies, but these are certainly not the most important characteristics of a leader. What does prior experience or a doctorate's degree tell us about the character and values of a person; what do these tell us about the ability of a person to connect with staff, to connect with the community, and—possibly the most important— to inspire principals and teachers to reach their goals? Prior experience as a superintendent and a sheepskin with a PhD after the name can be relatively poor indices of these qualities—it is necessary to judge the best candidate as a whole person, to dig below the surface, and look into the individual's value system. What courage, brains, and heart will this person bring to the job?

As we set out to conduct the national search in Wake County, we began to realize that we had some exemplary candidates in our midst— individuals who had worked in the school district, were experienced administrators, and were respected by their peers. In fact, we had one administrator who the four new board members felt would be an excellent choice for superintendent, but he did not have a doctorate's degree. The criterion for a doctorate's degree had always been on the list of attributes needed by superintendent candidates. Being full of enthusiasm for new approaches to doing business, the four new board members approached another board member with just two years experience and advocated for the idea that if an existing administrator was interested in the job, we should make it possible to conduct an internal search first. Further, these four argued that the criterion for an advanced degree should be secondary to hiring the most qualified individual—a person who could move the school district forward in the direction that the board wanted.

In the *Wizard of Oz* story, when the Scarecrow finally asks the Wizard for his brain, he is given a diploma and the degree "ThD" (Doctor of Thinkology). The Wizard, poking fun at the emphasis on sheepskins rather than knowledge, insists that people who attend universities think deep thoughts with no more brains than what the Scarecrow has—the only difference being the diploma and the degree. L. Frank Baum, then, would have approved of our eliminating the requirement of a doctorate.

Subsequently, we did conduct an internal search first, we did set aside the criterion for a doctorate's degree, and we did hire the individual whom many of us believed was a superb candidate. Bill McNeal was the only internal applicant and he impressed the board so much in the hiring process that he became the consensus choice. Had we proceeded with a national search, Bill's lack of a doctorate's degree might have "blinded" the board to his many other assets, not least of which that he was established and accomplished in the school district.

Bill had extensive experience as a central office administrator, school principal, and teacher. With his knowledge of the school district, experience as an administrator, and many other attributes he brought to the job, the board of education believed it had hired an outstanding superintendent. This was later affirmed when Bill was named in 2004 the National Superintendent of the Year by the American Association of School Administrators.

During that search and hiring process, some in the community publicly ridiculed the board for allowing a candidate without a doctorate's degree to interview for the job. Further, how could we consider a candidate with no superintendent's experience to run what was then the twenty-fifth largest system in the country? (This criticism conveniently overlooked the fact that Bill had served for seven months as the district's interim superintendent.) What could we be thinking? While the critics claimed that we were being foolish or worse, we maintained we were actually being better stewards of the public's trust by initially limiting the search to internal candidates.

The school board wanted a proven leader with experience in community relations, as well as someone who would be a good communicator, would be trusted by principals and peers, and would be dedicated to the school district. Having worked in the school district as long as he had, everyone was familiar with Bill and knew that he had already been "tested" on these criteria.

An added benefit of choosing Bill was that when he retired in 2006, after six years at the helm, he had in his deputy superintendent a well-trained person available to assume the leadership mantle. All that would be needed was a board that would be willing to again take the heat of forgoing a national search to do an internal search first. In 2006, the board did carry out the internal search—with some of the same questioning by the public—and again the board selected the best candidate, the deputy superintendent Dr. Del Burns.

Rather than relying on assumed criteria of excellence, in its last two choices for superintendent, WCPSS has conducted education like a business, making the best decisions based on proven criteria. What better measure of a prospects' talents can there be than to know them personally and their work in the day-to-day operations of the school district? Certainly, national searches may be appropriate occasionally. But you do your district a disservice if you overlook the talent you have in your own district. And, don't be fooled by criteria that may have little basis in reality. From this perspective, WCPSS has acted like a business, setting aside the politics and the typical criteria to identify the candidate best suited to our interests, our community, and our vision for students. Further, it is expected that each superintendent will work to develop the district's future leadership, including the position of superintendent—what in business is called succession planning.

Every organization needs a succession plan and reliance on a national search every three to five years, lurching from one new superintendent to the next, is not a succession plan. True, there will be times when you want to hire the superintendent from outside for the qualities that he or she will bring to the position, but these qualities are often framed by the immediate and short-term contingencies that the board is facing at the time. In contract, succession planning is a necessary ingredient of long-term planning.[9]

Performance Criteria for the Superintendent

A very common business practice for many years has been to ensure that all employees' effort is aligned toward accomplishing the same vision, mission, goals, and strategies. Even public school systems have recognized this business practice and made it theirs as well. In our schools, the vision, mission, goals, and strategies look great on walls, in notebooks, brochures, and newsletters. However, unlike business where often a clear path to alignment exists, such as reduce-your-waste-increase-your-profit, in education the path is sometimes not so clear. For instance, what is the best strategy to teach a child to read? Certainly, there are a number of strategies depending on a variety of factors, and the issue of alignment becomes one of flexibly adapting to these factors. In education, getting all employees on the same page to accomplish that task takes some doing.

An even longer business practice has been to give employees annual performance appraisals or evaluations. These are done each year in writing by thousands of businesses, large ones more commonly than smaller businesses, with the intended benefit of improving individual performance and consequently that of the whole organization. In an environment like education, where alignment of mission, goals, objectives, and activities is not as clear cut as in a business that produces widgets, the performance evaluation is an important tool for monitoring and reinforcing alignment, and performance evaluations need to start at the top.

Prior to Bill McNeal's selection as superintendent, formal performance evaluations were seldom done for the WCPSS superintendent. They were performed consistently for other employees, but not the top person. As to why, we can only guess. For example, we did hear from one board member who said that if you put the criteria in writing, then the superintendent would only be responsible for those things and not other criteria that might also be important. If followed to its logical conclusion, this form of thinking would indicate that a board should list every possible criterion that can be imagined, but surely this is not what a board would want to do.

Of course, a superintendent's job description cannot spell out each and every possible performance criterion, with instructions for evaluating each. Such minutiae would actually eliminate the need for a superintendent and composing it would also be impossible. You can't have hundreds of criteria *and* have a useful evaluation, but you can have a well-defined set of criteria that collectively span the breadth of operations. And, a well-defined set of criteria can be reliably measured.

When Bill was hired as superintendent, the board set ten criteria with each directly tied to the board's goal and its underlying pillars (an example of the criteria that the board set for Bill's 2004 evaluation is provided in Appendix B).

He embraced this process because it allowed him to take those same criteria and hold his subordinates accountable for the same standards. Within a couple of years, alignment toward the board's goals had been accomplished with everyone from the superintendent to the custodial staff. Every employee understood how their job impacted the goals the board set for educating children and knew that they were being held personally responsible. At top levels of the organization, through at least the principals, everyone knew that their alignment with the board goals could be reflected in their paychecks. It is not surprising that continuous improvement in test scores followed.

After alignment is in place, the only breakdown that will occur is when supervisors do not implement the performance evaluation process properly through lack of training or follow through. This will happen in business and education, so paying lip service to alignment is not sufficient. It is necessary to also ensure that the evaluation process is functioning well and continues to support alignment. Evaluation requires monitoring the criteria in an objective fashion, noting the progress that is being made toward meeting the criteria, and meeting with the individual to discuss findings of the performance evaluation with praise for accomplishments and recommendations for improvements. When implemented well, alignment will support student achievement in a school district of any character or size.

Formal Performance Evaluations

There are all kinds of performance evaluations or appraisals. The one that makes the most impact is the annual one in writing, the kind that calls for the evaluator and evaluated to sign the evaluation. Big companies spend a lot of money trying to perfect these evaluation tools. Of course, the evaluation process will never be perfected but the effort is worthy. The benefit of the employee performance evaluation is not in the form itself. Rather, the benefit is in the evaluation process that starts with alignment of the organization's goals to the evaluation measurement. Whether the measurement ratings are numerical or alphabetical does not matter, so long as the rating clearly reveals whether the goals have been accomplished or not. Further, this evaluation needs to make clear what needs to be improved in the future, if anything.

Following the evaluation measurement, employer and employee must meet to explain and discuss the evaluation. All of these elements are critically important to making the process work. In some companies, the managers never seem to make time for these meetings because other pressing items take precedence. Not devoting the necessary time to the evaluation meeting is certainly a detriment to improvement.

In education, the evaluation of the superintendent requires that the board be diligent. In WCPSS, the board put into the superintendent's contract that he must receive his performance evaluation and new criteria within sixty days of the end of the school year or an automatic raise would kick in. Imagine, a board specifying a criterion by which its own work might be measured! Even though the sixty-day criterion meant the board had to work hard on the evaluation during the summer, no board member wanted to suffer from the local media picking up on our failure to do our duty and causing an automatic increase at taxpayer expense. We never missed our deadline.

Every year we spent many hours collecting evaluation comments from stakeholders and all board members and compiling them into valuable feedback for the superintendent. Every year the evaluation criteria were fine-tuned to reflect our current goals and where we needed to be headed as a school district. Did this process make the superintendent a better superintendent? Yes, without question. Did he become a better manager of his staff from implementing this process? Of course he did.

Did alignment occur? Did Wake County's results keep improving? Did national recognition follow? Yes, yes, and yes.

We make no claim that our success in WCPSS is due solely to the superintendent, nor solely to our evaluation practices. The personnel evaluation is a typical business practice that, when placed in service along with others, yielded measurable results and tremendous success. The larger the organization, the more important it is that this system be formalized, that training be conducted every year on how to conduct the evaluation effectively, and that there be follow-up to ensure evaluations are being done. Even in a small school system, the process will pay big dividends as early as the first year. And the benefits will continue to grow.

WHAT YOU CAN DO TO IMPROVE

- Evaluate your internal possibilities for leadership before going national
- Be sure your current superintendent is developing qualified successors
- Set measurable performance criteria as a part of the formal evaluations for school district leaders
- Get out in the community to build loyalty

ORGANIZING YOUR LEADERSHIP

The bigger your business or school district, the more leaders you will have. Some will be generalists, such as a chief of staff who supports the superintendent, and some will be specialists, such as the chief business officer. Whether in business or education, these subordinate leaders are critically important to how well the organization functions. Do you select these leaders for their loyalty to you, for their particular talents, or according to some other criteria? Probably, the best approach is to have a mix with some you know you can trust in confidence and some you know who won't hesitate to argue with you. Regardless of the mix you select, you will need to organize your leadership, and doing this well may be the critical element in whether you have a well functioning team.

Superintendent's Cabinet

Like any good business, the higher the quality of top level leadership, the greater the chances of success. It is extremely important that individuals who will fill the upper echelons be chosen for their skills, experiences, and ability to work as a team. Good interpersonal and communication skills should be an absolute requirement and non-negotiable. Moreover, you are seeking innovative, can-do individuals who share your passion for all students' academic success. And they must be loyal and willing to subvert their ego for the common good, yet willing to tell their boss what they think and stand on principle when they are in the right. Whether in business or education, these individuals may not be the most senior person on your staff.

This team will spend many hours together discussing strategy and the best approach to achieve the agreed upon objectives. Specialists should be sought in the areas of instruction, operations/facilities, human resources, finance, communication, student services, evaluation/research, and varied other roles. Each area represents a specific segment of the school district requiring an expert in that area as division head. As division head, these leaders are expected to be able to select, organize, direct, and hold subordinate staff accountable. The school system's and superintendent's professional well-being depend on the ability of these leaders to run their areas efficiently.

When meeting with the leadership cabinet, the superintendent should be knowledgeable enough to ask the right questions and tough enough to ask the hard questions. Playing devil's advocate is a good way to determine if an idea has been well thought out or is a work in progress. You must insist that you get quality intelligence at all times regardless of the problems that lie ahead. Never shy away from bad news and be willing to make the hard call—this is leadership. If a cabinet member gives you partial information or spins it to make it look better, the superintendent needs to press for full disclosure. If obfuscation or spin continues, then the superintendent needs to consider having a conference with the person or even seeking a replacement. While it is always difficult to transfer an individual or let someone go, doing so for the right reasons—that you want leaders willing to argue for the truth when confident of being right and willing to acknowledge problems when they are evident—will stand you in good stead with your remaining staff.

Your cabinet of senior staff members needs to operate very much like a family, with loyalty to the head of the family. This doesn't mean that they follow blindly, but all do their part to help the organization flourish. If they are people of principle, they will try to do the right thing even if it is unpopular and the superintendent may not agree. Principled, competent senior staffers should be cherished and supported. Support should come in the form of autonomy, positive personal feedback, and public recognition when superior work is done. Staff members should not be chastised publicly by their boss when there is some question about their performance. Probing questions about performance, competence, and experiences should be handled in private and followed up in writing. Never try to embarrass, ridicule, or humiliate a member of the team. Praise publicly; admonish privately.

There should be very clear goals and objectives so that all team members can be on the same page. In fact, it is wise for the team to help create these goals and objectives, thereby providing ownership. Time must be devoted to planning for the team; hopefully, this planning can be done at a location away from the work environment, preferably starting in the morning to take advantage of fresh thinking. Allow casual dress for these planning meetings; this is hard work and comfortable dress will help everyone summon the energy they will need. Hire a facilitator who will encourage all members of the team to participate. With the facilitator leading the group, the superintendent can sit with the group as an equal. One person, one vote should rule the day. If, at the end of the day, consensus cannot be found on an issue, then the superintendent may weigh in with a decision.

The School Board Chairperson

What is the job of a school board chairperson? Ask that question of a hundred people and you will likely receive that many answers. For us, the correct answer is that the job should be viewed as the same as a chair of the board for any large business; hire the right CEO (superintendent), properly supervise her or him, and manage the other board members. Unfortunately for superintendents around the country, some board chairs do not operate this way. Rather, the role of board chair becomes confused with that of the superintendent, raising the question of whether the board chair or the superintendent is the principle spokesperson for the school system. Our answer is that only one person can be in charge, speaking for and leading the system, and that is the superintendent.

The school board chair needs to function more like a business board chair—in the background. An effective board that works well together is of great benefit to a superintendent and school system. That can only happen with a very effective chair who manages the board members well. These board members are elected officials. They have earned their spot on the campaign trail with no expectation of money or fame. They must represent their electorate, and the board chair must appreciate their individuality while trying to meld their voices for a common purpose.

Most boards will be comprised of a collection of independent-minded and good-hearted citizens who may have different agendas. This reality is what makes the chair position so critical. The board chair needs to be someone who can work behind the scenes helping individual board members accomplish their goals while also striving to keep the group together in achieving the system goals. Managing the board is the most important job of the chair after the superintendent is hired. A board chair who can accomplish those tasks is the superintendent's MVP. And, one who cannot do that is of little value to the school district. If the chair cannot manage the board, the superintendent must, and it can result in a dysfunctional system.

Unfortunately, many board chairs do not have this understanding of their job and role in the school district. Rather, they may think of themselves as the front person for the system, the media, the principals, and the teachers. They are proud of their schools and want to be the spokesperson. However, all this does is confuse the public about who is really in charge. The leader should be the superintendent, not the board chair or the board. To do otherwise confuses the community and exposes the board chair and the superintendent to the potential of miscommunication or, even worse, open conflict.

Independently elected boards with effective board chairs, who understand that their job is to facilitate the work of the board members while also providing supervision of the superintendent, are rare indeed.

Business People on the School Board

Most people will tell you that there is no more thankless public office than the school board. It is an office to avoid, especially for those with other political aspirations. Traditionally in North Carolina, school boards consist of public school advocates who presently have or have had children in the schools and who have probably served for many years on parent-teacher organizations. Generally, we're sure that it is true that school board members love children and want to do what is best for them. Perhaps because, in North Carolina, board members have no ability to levy taxes, this role rarely attracts business people. In Wake County, business people just did not want to commit the time it took to provide this public service. With only a few exceptions, this had been true until the day Tom Oxholm was elected to the board.

In 1999, Wake County was very fortunate to add a certified public accountant to our board of education. Tom brought to the board table his CPA and chief financial officer's experience from the business world. He immediately helped the district see that by implementing business practices in the day-to-day operations of the district, our effectiveness and efficiency would improve. We upgraded our school improvement planning process by focusing more on measuring results, we became more data-driven and committed to continuous improvement, and we improved our marketing and budgeting processes—the latter included preparing business plans.

Tom helped the district streamline budget documents so that they were understandable not only to accountants, the school board, and the county commissioners, but also to the person on the street. He also brought tremendous credibility to the table when we engaged in budget negotiations with the county commissioners. Consequently, our overall image improved in the business community specifically, and in the community generally. Tom is an example of how business leadership can bring new perspectives to a school board.

In education, one measure of courage is seeking new and challenging perspectives, and we maintain that school districts must become proactive at encouraging our business counterparts to participate on school boards. If no business people are on the school board, the superintendent needs to convene a committee of financial experts from the community to advise the board and superintendent on the "business of education." It cannot be a committee for appearances only, because business people will not continue to serve if they believe their purpose is only to convince the public that there is some financial oversight. School leaders must appreciate that business members will want to tackle the substantive issues and questions even if outside their realm of experience or training. It will be surprising the degree to which the business member wants to understand curriculum. For their investment of time and effort, the work of such a committee should be respected and publicized. In turn, the school system will get good ideas on how to improve, and the public's respect for the district's effort to be accountable will increase in proportion to the involvement of business leaders.

In 1999, Tom ran for the school board with a great deal of peer pressure. He had not wanted to run for public office of any kind. Business friends talked him into it, citing reasons such as the financial strength it would add to the board and the improved perception of the board by the business community. During the campaign, Tom talked with many folks, both school supporters and critics. One theme was very clear to him and to the others running at the same time for the board: The community perceived that the school board was not interested in what the public thinks. Although the board had numerous ways for the general public, the business community, and parents to communicate with them, the common perception was that the board was not listening.

Tom understood that this perception could derive from a "bunker mentality" that board members might project, in part because the school system was always under attack. To the public, the board and top administrators appeared to prefer to engage in taking cover versus opening up the doors. After Tom was elected and had had some time to learn the operations, he recognized another explanation for apparent tight-lipped, inattentive board members. School board members have access to voluminous information about school operations and personnel, and spend hundreds—if not thousands—of hours learning about schools and how they are run. Parents and the public have limited access to this information and are usually interested chiefly in one subject—their child. Thus, the board members may smile when the individual member of the public speaks, but may also believe this person is representing personal interests. Consciously or unconsciously, the board member could be projecting an image of not listening—smiling but not agreeing. What the board member may not appreciate is how the individual wants to know that her or his opinion counts, that this opinion is being considered in an equitable fashion with other public opinions.

Before 2000, our board had several committees, but every board member was interested enough in each committee's work so that any committee meeting usually ended up being a "Committee of the Whole" meeting. Because of this cumbersome way of doing business, in January 2000, the individual committee meetings were made a part of the board meetings. You can imagine one outcome of this move—hours and hours of discussion. The first three board meetings under this structure went from 4 p.m. to 1 a.m. Meetings this long, especially public meetings, are dysfunctional and accomplish little.

With that as a background, a different structure for the board and its committees was proposed: First, that board members be assigned to two or three committees each and be expected to attend their designated meetings. They could attend other committee meetings if they desired. A committee's report would be brought to a board meeting but no action was required until the board met at the next meeting to follow. That way, all members would have sufficient time to understand the work and proposals of the committee before any votes would be taken. Most importantly, each committee was entrusted by the entire board to develop their proposals with the understanding that these would be brought before the entire board for consideration and debate. The committees would need to do their homework.

Then another proposal was made. This second proposal called for the board to appoint citizens to serve on the committees as well. This was innovative but some thought it was preaching anarchy, stating something like, "We were elected to make the decisions, not other citizens. This is our job; we can't delegate it." The board chair at the time refused to even discuss the idea in a meeting. Not until a year later, at a board retreat, was this structure presented for discussion. Tom explained how it would work and responded to questions and concerns. By the following summer, the board was willing to try it with Tom's finance committee and see how it worked.

No other school board in the state had tried this approach to the degree that WCPSS was considering. This was new thinking and untested. But very shortly, the benefits were undeniable. The public was informed that citizens were participating in board decisions and the walls were coming down. Citizens actually did participate and spread the word that they had input. The board received many, many good ideas as well as a sense of the public's opinion on important issues from these citizens. And, citizens with an interest in school progress received both information and leadership training for potential future board service. In fact, the person who took Tom's place on the board in 2003 served on one of these first board committees.

Initially skeptical board members were able to observe how well the finance committee worked. Six months after trying this with the finance committee, the board expanded the structure to all committees, and our committees worked that way for the rest of Tom's term on the board. Just to clarify, these committees were not making decisions for the school system. They were thoroughly discussing issues and making recommendations to the board on the issues. The citizens attended the meetings, did their homework, gave their opinions, and voted when called for. But they did not have the final say. As indicated, the committees would make a report to the board and the board was the elected vehicle that subsequently voted on any proposals made by the committees. In fact, many of the committee recommendations were approved by the board, but certainly not all.

Conducting committee meetings in a business-like manner contributed to the success of these committees. The committees functioned like committees in other corporate and nonprofit groups with a business agenda. A business-like way of running the committee meetings was beneficial for the citizen members and board members alike, some of whom had never run a committee meeting. Each committee had its issues developed at an annual board retreat, and each committee had to report to the board as it accomplished its challenges over the course of the year. The business of the board was getting done effectively and efficiently. The public was participating. Future board members were being trained. The business of education was getting done.

Superintendent's Finance Committee

The superintendent also had his own finance committee. In 1997, the WCPSS operating budget was almost $500 million. That's a lot of money to be accountable for, and even though the district's expenditures were below national average on a per-pupil basis, communicating the efficiency of our operations to a skeptical public was a challenge. (This challenge will become increasingly more difficult in the future as the 2007–08 budget exceeds $1 billion due to the growth in students and inflation.)

The superintendent is most often an educator by experience and training. Typically, the superintendent's administrative cabinet members are educators as well. To whom can the superintendent look for good, independent advice on business practices such as budgeting and accounting? Because of this concern, McNeal set up a superintendent's finance committee to give him advice on financial matters, opinions when he was looking for new ideas on how to communicate about an issue, and critical perspectives on the public's financial criticisms of the school district. The finance committee, comprised of local chief financial officers (CFOs) of well known companies, provided what he needed along with increased credibility in the public's eyes and the eyes of the county commissioners (a major provider of school operating funds).

McNeal could call on this group for monthly meetings, or as needed, and used the group for various matters in his term as superintendent. The business people were glad to provide the service. They learned as much or more than they gave in advice. Away from the finance committee, they were able to lead informed discussions of school finances with other business leaders and their respective chambers of commerce. They also contributed to the financial success of the system. Any school district would benefit from this kind of citizen's "business" committee. All it takes is an open-minded superintendent with a nothing-to-hide attitude in his approach to managing the school district's financial records.

A recommendation of the consultants involved in the investigation of the district's transportation fraud (we discuss this event in detail later in the book) was to ask these CFOs to serve on the school system's external audit committee. In general, an audit committee approves the internal audit plan for the year, reviews those reports, and works with the external auditors during their annual audit process. A committee of school board members without much business experience will not be of much help in this way. But, an audit committee that consists of community CFOs provides a much better functioning committee due to their expertise, and also lends great credibility to the process and committee.

About the Principal's Leadership

Clearly, the superintendent's role is to be a leader. In this role, the superintendent can inspire principals and teachers to greater achievement, and the children and the community will be the beneficiaries of this inspiration. In business, key managers are inspired in a number of ways—compensation, benefits, travel perks, stock options, etc. But in education, many of these "inspirational" motivators are not available to the superintendent. For the superintendent, much of his inspiration of others comes down to recognizing and praising the personal enrichment that is earned by achieving common goals.

When McNeal became superintendent in 2000, the school board's performance criteria for the superintendent held him accountable for improving test scores and closing the achievement gap to reach Goal 2003. To do so, McNeal had two main alternatives available to him: reallocate resources that were already scarce and inspire principals and teachers to reach new heights of performance. It was necessary to do both. Funds and programs were realigned to refocus monies and energies where they could be most effective, and school principals were tasked to aspire for higher achievement gains.

By focusing many communication and training efforts on school principals, as business does with its managers, it was possible to distribute the effort throughout the school district. The superintendent had his charge from the board and the principals had their charge from the superintendent. The superintendent could make it clear that he and the principals had the same goal and the same metric, and the superintendent had limited ability to offer the incentive of higher paying contracts for principals who were able to produce.

Without question, pay is not the chief motivator for our quality principals. If pay alone were the motivator, many of today's principals could be earning much higher salaries in another field of work. Still, along with the pat on the back, the occasional recognition, honor or award, and the thanks that principals receive from students, parents, and teachers, it is nice to be able to put something extra in the paycheck when a job is well done.

Among many examples in WCPSS, there are three principals that come to mind when we think of a job well done. The three principals each faced different situations at their schools, but all three were relentlessly determined to make a difference and to do so for every child at the school. These three principals held themselves personally accountable for the success of their staff and students.

At one elementary school, located in a working class community with more than 50 percent of its children living in low-income families, a new principal was hired that came from another school district. This person inspired the search committee with her attention to detail and ability to connect with the school community. As a principal, she was extremely focused, supported her team, and able to build a culture of high expectations. For principal and staff alike, there was an atmosphere of no excuses. The principal saw to it that her teachers developed professionally, ensuring that all were made aware of best practices and research using data to drive instruction. Along with her staff, this principal viewed parents as partners and saw to it that they too understood their clearly defined roles. Whereas before, parents may not have been seen as significant collaborators in the educational process, this principal opened the school to the community, operating on the belief that strong schools exist in strong communities. No child was to be left behind and the school has subsequently earned the numbers to prove it.

At another elementary school located in a middle-class to slightly above middle-class community, there was a veteran, no nonsense principal who required that creativity and innovation be the hallmark of the school's program. This individual was not satisfied with the tried-and-true; rather, this individual was constantly on the lookout for the next cutting edge improvement. This veteran was one of the first principals to contract with a curriculum program focused on data analysis to drive instruction. In this particular school they had one of the narrowest achievement gaps in the county. All students—regardless of their socio-economic status, race, gender, or handicapping condition—*all students*, excelled. In fact, it was in this school where it was realized that they did one of the best jobs educating African American males, a population group that is often seen to lag the furthest behind other population groups. Along with curricular improvements, the school infused character education across the curriculum with the expectation that students would respect self, others, and the staff. They succeeded in turning the school into a home—just like a large family with the expectation that all of the children would rise academically with the appropriate support of school and home. School took on many of the positive characteristics of home for the children. This school received numerous awards and was constantly on the visitation list of many dignitaries.

At a third elementary school, located in a middle- to upper-income area, the school had a unique distinction that the student body as a whole was achieving at high levels. The school did have a small number of poor children and minorities, with some of them not achieving well, but the greater number of students performed well enough to keep the school in the top ranks. In a situation like this, it could be easy to forget the small number of students not doing well, and it could also be easy to think that the students who were performing well had nothing to gain. Instead, this principal was not satisfied and showed that all students could make gains every year. Academically gifted students were expected to have high growth as were special education students. The belief of this particular leader was clear—it is not satisfactory to rest on our laurels. Regardless of where the student was at with achievement, the staff were not satisfied and continued to strive for excellence, taking each and every student to the next level by offering everyone a challenging classroom experience. Similarly, teachers were expected to perform at a high level or the expectation was that you wouldn't remain on that faculty, and some teachers did leave. Still, this principal was highly respected by the faculty as a whole, parents, and students. All knew that the principal cared deeply about their welfare and wanted to provide them with a great future.

These are only three examples and, by choice, they are all drawn from among elementary school principals for comparison purposes. There are many examples of middle school and high school principals in WCPSS with the same mix of these characteristics. Looking across the three principals, there were three different leadership styles, but what they had in common was Heart, because they truly cared about all children; Courage to expect the best, demand the best, and settle for nothing less; and Brains because all three believed in doing their homework, searching out the innovative techniques, and checking the data to see what progress was being made. And, all three principals understood how important it is to create the feeling of Home where staff, students, and parents all felt wanted and shared the same passion for achievement.

It is tempting to join the academicians who research and debate the characteristics of principal leadership. However, the effort to qualify and quantify any single list of these characteristics is ultimately doomed to failure. Leadership is a unique characteristic, and we will simply say that the effective principal will demonstrate courage, brains, and heart while creating the home-away-from-home at school.

WHAT YOU CAN DO TO IMPROVE

- Hire leaders with the expertise, skills, *and* value system that tell you they are committed to the best for *every* child
- Involve your leaders in many opportunities for training and decision making
- Create the opportunities for each leader to "own" the process, program, and/or outcome
- Don't overlook how school board members could also benefit from leadership training
- Seek out the advice and consultation of business leaders—they will not be hesitant to offer you their opinions and may even step up to help
- Involve citizens on school board committees
- Form a superintendent's finance committee
- Eliminate principal tenure (or imagine the possibility) and establish incentives for performance

COMMUNICATING WITH YOUR PUBLIC

Businesses spend a lot of time and money trying to communicate effectively with the public. This effort is expensive but worth the cost. Getting your message out to a public that isn't really listening is why we have advertising, marketing, and careers in public relations. Communicating with your public is a challenge that never ends and is constantly changing. For public schools, compounding this challenge is the fact that school districts have very little money that they can devote to this task. Still, the education leader will be remiss to ignore or give communications too little attention.

Community Involvement by the Superintendent

A significant indicator of strong leadership is a willingness to reach out and significantly engage stakeholders. In the field of education, the community represents very important stakeholder groups, and engagement includes full participation of these stakeholders in decision making. In turn, participation in decision making better ensures that the public and stakeholders are educated on the issues of the day.

One definition of a community is a group of people holding common interests living in a particular area. In our case, the community is the school district—representing the entire county. Within this community, we know that there is agreement on a number of issues. One major area of agreement, where parents are concerned, is academic success for their children and, by extension, academic success for all children. This community of people is unified around striving for academic excellence and through this community we find there is a culture of high expectations for the school district.

Having a community that is knowledgeable and involved, made up of a group of people with common academic interests and high expectations, is extremely important. After the community becomes involved in the activities and culture of the school district, a number of positive things begin to happen. They begin to understand the dynamics of the school system; who the key players are; why certain policies, procedures, and regulations exist; and the cultural norms of the school system. Essentially, the community takes ownership—an important business concept for success.

As you are well aware, every good-sized business dedicates much of its leadership time to involvement in the community through chambers of commerce, charity boards, United Way, study committees, visiting lectures, etc. Why would a business devote this much energy to something that seemingly doesn't make money? Well, it does make money for the business—just not in the direct way of sales, but in the indirect way of establishing, sustaining, and enhancing the business identity.

Furthermore, involvement in the community like this often leads to new ideas and business opportunities. Involving stakeholders from your community in your work is no less important for the education leader.

The involvement of community stakeholders also helps to shape, define, and refine the school district. Through community involvement, we find that our school leaders start to understand their clientele, what the clientele expect, what they do not expect, and what they truly value. Having an opportunity to work directly with community groups makes better leaders, because the leaders now start to understand why their clients believe as they do and what they are likely to support.

What form should community involvement take among school leaders? Actually, it can take several forms. One is a willingness to go out and speak to numerous groups: PTAs, advisory councils, faith communities, civic organizations, business leaders, and students. The key is making certain that you know the major groups that make up your community of stakeholders. Some of these groups are very supportive of the schools and the district. Other groups may be moderately supportive and, of course, some groups do not support the schools or school district. In some cases, the nonsupportive groups may even campaign against the school district.

How do you discern which groups to speak to? The answer is to speak to as many diverse groups as possible. As you speak to groups—supportive or nonsupportive—the message should be the same even if it is delivered differently. You could begin with some personal anecdotes based on your research of the group, how their children are doing relative to the whole, and what could be done to assist them even more. The mission, goals, objectives, and strategies of the district and individual schools should be reported like a mantra.

When describing the areas that need improvement, be ready to explain what can be done to make the needed improvements, the plans for implementation, and how the plan might be accessible to the community. Provide the community with documentation indicating the performance of students, the dropout rate, the graduation rate, the attendance rate, and parent, teacher, and student survey data. Talk about the facilities and repair needs that surface from time to time, be it paint or major renovations or the need for a playground or additional technology—things you know will enhance teaching, learning, and student safety. All these indicators provide information that can be used in helping the community understand what the district is doing well and which areas need improvement. Do not be hesitant to identify the areas needing improvement.

Many of the groups that are the most accessible to address are those tied directly to the school district. However, in most school districts, approximately 30 percent of the adults in the community have school-aged children; the other 70 percent do not. Therefore, a number of groups may not be on the district's mailing list. Those groups must still be addressed. They can be found in their places of worship, in senior citizen communities, in civic and social groups. If community members are not directly involved in your schools, still, they must be sought out and brought into the communication circle. Remember, everyone has a vote. Even without children in school, these are the people that you want to be advocates for the school district when it is time to rally support of a school district's building program or for carrying out the strategies necessary for additional funding. Although they may have no children in the school system, as community members, they should understand that the community's children are tomorrow's employees and managers. It behooves everyone to have well-educated citizens, whether it is the restaurant employee who takes your order correctly, the civil engineer who builds a bridge that won't collapse, or the head of the chamber of commerce who knows how to attract new revenue for the community.

Being ready to speak before all of these individuals and groups takes courage, and doing so better ensures stakeholder participation in decision making and subsequent support for public education.

Working With the Media

Your home or place of business will have an address, a location, and an identity. So too should your school district and schools, and working closely with your local media is one means by which you make it known that your home is a desirable place to live.

In business, the media provide a vehicle for advancing public relations and for developing your "brand" recognition. Businesses establish a brand and then work to promote brand name recognition for their business. Who isn't familiar with the Nike swoosh, the AFLAC duck, or the Geico gecko? The ability to develop a brand name, control your message, select your audience, and communicate your message as you desire are characteristics of successful businesses. The same is true for public education. You want your brand to be about excellence for all and higher standards of academic achievement. How you work with the media and manage public relations in your district will determine in no small measure how well you will be accepted as a leader in your school district or your school—one who is advancing excellence and achievement.

Public relations can mean the difference between a successful bond referendum and failure; strong or weak support from your parental community; and pride, shame, or indifference in your school district among the students, teachers, parents, and the community at large.

We must admit that we did not always have an appreciation for how important public relations were to our school district. In earlier days, working with the media was often seen as a chore and we were not good at it. Rather than anticipating media inquiries, we made excuses for ourselves when surprised by the interest the media would take in an event or issue. Rather than being prepared in advance, we often had to chase down information. Rather than being able to present all the information in context, we often overlooked the important details that added clarity to our message. Rather than appearing confident and knowledgeable, we often appeared confused—or worse, deceptive. We were well intentioned; we just weren't good at working with the media. Our brand name recognition was confused, if existent at all.

Recognizing this problem, we borrowed another page from business and moved to upgrade our communications division. We realized how essential it is to find the right skill set in a communications director and these skills are not ones that educators commonly possess. Most teachers, principals, and superintendents can probably remember taking a college course in public speaking, but how many of us have made a career of working with the media? Hiring a talented person from within the organization may not provide you with this skill set, and in our case, we looked outside our organization to find the person we wanted. The person we sought was an individual who understood public relations and the media, and who had enough self-confidence and experience to maneuver and change the attitude of senior staff.

Because we knew that the communications director would need to be a "take-charge" type of person, we realized that the person we hired would need to report directly to the superintendent. The communications director needed to have access to the superintendent any time of the day, as well as access to all offices and all meetings, open sessions and closed sessions. Clearly, the organization's leaders should be on top of the issues of the day and so too should the communications director. Additionally, through having this person report to the superintendent, we were able to emphasize how necessary it was for staff to listen and respond to this expert talent. It is of interest to note that we recruited this individual from business.

With a communications director in place, we empowered this individual to teach us how to work with the media. For a training activity, we once viewed an episode of *The Bob Newhart Show*, with Bob's psychologist character going on a popular TV show to discuss his practice. Before going live, the host of the show engaged Bob in light chit chat, and gave Bob the impression that he would get a chance to tout his business and his successes. This would be an opportunity for Bob to help the community know what he does and that he was very successful in his profession. Can you see yourself in this role? Wouldn't it be great to get on television and tell the community about what a good job administrators and teachers are doing in the school district or at your school?

The first question the host asked was, "Why is it that you haven't healed anyone?" Followup questions were ones such as, "Why do you charge so much if you haven't healed anyone?" "Why doesn't the public know about the sociopath that you are protecting?" Put yourself in Bob's place: "Why is it that you can't teach all children to read at grade level?" "Why is it that you have students dropping out of school?" "Why should we educate the children of illegal immigrants?" "Why repair the rundown city schools when you can build new schools in the suburbs?"

If you know Bob Newhart's acting style, you know how flustered he was by the host's questioning and how he stumbled with his responses. He mumbled and had no good response to the host's questions, which would prompt the host to bore in with more questions. It gets pretty hot for Bob. This was a fun activity and yet it also delivered a powerful message. Is it that you can't trust the media? No, actually, the lesson is that you need to understand the media and be prepared, which in education means staying on your message to get your point across and share new information.

Following the Bob Newhart video, we viewed another video providing a contrasting example of how to work with the media. In this second video, there had been a plane crash and several people were killed. A vice president of the airline was to speak with the media and knew there would be tough questions. This person had been trained in media relations and understood how important it was for him to express sympathy with the families of the deceased. He knew also that it would be important to explain what the airline was doing to provide families with the latest information.

While the context of these two videos is quite different—one dealing with issues seemingly much less serious than the other—the lesson we gained from watching the contrasting videos was to be confident with your message and be prepared for tough questions. You should anticipate the tough questions; you should expect them; and you should *want* to address them. This we expected of our communications director. We wanted this person to be articulate and sensitive to the public's concerns, to be prepared and ready to stay on message, and to be an educator who would in turn help us develop the mentality and skills to handle the tough questions.

Employing a communications director and watching videos that contrast different communication styles will not be sufficient to teach you the attitude and skills for working with the media. We also brought in national and local media consultants to train our top level administrators to deal with the media. We found some of the best resources to be the local media personalities whom we most often met on the other side of the microphone. One of these local consultants helped us understand that we don't have to answer all the questions, especially if we don't know the answer. Don't make something up and don't throw out data that could come back and haunt you. It's okay to say, "Let me get back to you with the answer." This individual also helped us to appreciate that it's okay to question the interviewer, "Where did you get your facts?" Generally speaking, you will be better informed than the media person and you shouldn't let irrelevant or inaccurate information go unchallenged.

We also learned how the media person will frequently ask the same question four different ways; when this happens, give the same answer four different times. You don't need to be intimidated, nor should you become upset at the redundancy—although you might point out that you are pleased to answer their question again. Also, our consultant emphasized that you need to know your reporters—not just their names, but their styles and their history of reporting on your district or school.

Finally, understand that what you say is never off the record. Everything you say counts. If the reporters don't write about your off-the-record comments this time around, you should know that they will remember your comments and this information may show up sometime or somewhere else.

As we became increasingly skilled at working with the media, our beliefs evolved. We recognized the public's right to know and their right to complete and timely information. We want to respond to the media as quickly as possible; we want to provide full and accurate information; we're not interested in dodging questions or adding hyperbole and spin to the information we're sharing. Moreover, we want to provide this information in a coordinated and responsible fashion.

The most sensitive time you will face the media is when tragedy strikes, for instance, the suicide of a student or death of staff or student by vehicular accident. For fast-breaking and emotionally laden news like this, one of the ways we would operate was to set up a media communications post. This would be a place where the media could converge and everyone could get the same information at the same time. The location should not be at the school if the incident is associated with a particular school. Along with the communications director, we would make the organization's leaders available. At a time of tragedy, this person at the school level is the principal and at the district level is the superintendent. For instance, when we lost four students in a car accident following a ball game, the community needed to see the face of the superintendent and know the school was grieving for these students with their parents.

As well as tragedies, for major issues such as student reassignment, we make the superintendent available to the media; however, the superintendent need not always be the spokesperson. Who is the most informed and most prepared? In some cases, this could be the communications director, or a division leader or the school principal.

Media outlets are multifaceted, including television, newspapers, Internet, webcasts, blogs, wikis, flyers, brochures, newsletters, speaking engagements, and journal articles—to name some of the common forms. As a leader, you should make use of all such media outlets, although you may have a different purpose for each. Obviously, you want to maintain a steady flow of information about your district and school. It's better to have a well-informed public that is educated on the latest issues and prepared at any time to make educated decisions about the issues than it is to have a public that will make decisions based on another person's inter-pretation or political agenda. Build relations to all of these media outlets.

Interestingly, having a strong relationship with all forms of media out-lets serves your organization in ways other than just providing informa-tion. Having a strong relationship with diverse media outlets affords you opportunities to counter bad publicity that any particular outlet may be putting out. You don't have to depend on a single outlet for your media communications. Media outlets like to get the scoop on each other, and you can sometimes control the order in which you speak to these outlets. Rather than the newspaper reporter, you might first share your informa-tion with the radio reporter or the regional weekly. When you're a little angry with one, you spend time with the other. In many situations, you have the opportunity to decide who's going to get the story first and you can decide which media outlet you will call back first. School leaders should not forget that they have some controls in their relations with the media.

Having said all this, let's appreciate that working with the media will be one of your challenges. Without question, be open, honest, and under control. Practice before meeting with the media and be prepared. Don't be cornered. If all of your practice fails and you're hit with that question that you're not ready for, there are still strategies to keep in mind. For instance, you can explain that you haven't determined all the facts of the issue and that the question is being investigated. If you use this strategy, be prepared to offer another time when you can get back with the reporter to respond more fully.

Sometimes you will know that you are being invited to an event only so the host can showcase your inadequacies or failures. With a media set-up, the idea is to bring you into the arena and feast on you. One school of thought would ask, "If you know that's the case, why go?" But, another school of thought sees the opportunity. This opportunity is almost cer-tainly not with your reporter or your interviewer or your panel. Rather, it's with your audience. You're not going to convince all of your opponents of your message, but a significant number of your audience may be trying to make up their minds. By bringing your message out in this forum, you are able to demonstrate your belief in the truth of your position. Regardless of how emotional the program host may become, you remain cool, on message, and answer the questions as best you can. By showing up, having done your homework, and being ready to respond to the challenges, you also send a message about yourself and your leadership. Further, by meeting with a group of school critics, you certainly cannot lose supporters—you stand to gain them.

Here are a couple of personal examples. Invited to attend a meeting of the Wake Taxpayers Association, as superintendent, I (Bill) knew this was a total set-up. These folks were always trying to show how wasteful the school district was and that our requests for additional funding were unnecessary; however, I was confident that I could define some of the terms of the engagement. My first stipulation was that I would be first on the program and when I was done I would leave. Being first and leaving when finished would reduce the panelists' opportunities to engage the audience in an argument with me. Before the event, I spent time with my staff and anticipated what we thought I would be asked. On the appointed time, I showed up with facts and figures but spoke extemporaneously. I knew our facts were better than theirs. I stayed an hour and a half, answered every question, rebutted much of the information they were putting out, and then I left. I believe I helped make our case for some in the audience who were trying to make up their minds and showed that I was not intimated by the rhetoric. Four people followed me out the door and told me that they were very impressed.

On another occasion when I would be going on television to debate with an opponent of the school system, we found a number of videotapes of this individual and studied his style. What we saw was that he frequently used data to back up his outrageous statements, but his data were often wrong. Knowing that this person would throw some numbers at me, I was ready. When he would cite a particular statistic, I didn't try to explain how his figures were wrong; instead, I asked him where he got his figures. Because I knew the correct figures, I was confident that this challenge of mine would confuse him and I was ready to explain to him what the correct figures were.

Speaking of criticism, if you are married, you should appreciate that your spouse may be the best critic you can have when it comes to helping you deal with the media. As superintendent, I would often be upset about something said in an article when my wife, Faye, would find something else in the article that was complimentary to the school district. When speaking before a group, my wife would often attend and sit in the audience. Early in my talk, she would catch my eye and she'd let me know how I was doing, in the way that only a spouse can do.

The set-ups and biased perspectives are easy to recognize and relatively easy to counter, but it can be difficult to be objective about the general media coverage you receive. If the story or report is not completely and enthusiastically supportive of the schools, there is a tendency to concentrate on the negative and overlook the positive.

There was a time when we felt one reporter was being especially biased in his coverage and this individual worked for a major news outlet in the region. When we would confront this individual about his flawed reporting, an incredulous look would come over his face and he'd tell us that he had reported the story to the best of his ability. Eventually, we questioned ourselves. Did we have tunnel vision? Were we overly focused on the negative? We hired a consulting firm to conduct a six-month retrospective review of the news stories by this reporter. They wrote a report and said that, overall, we were getting positive press; we were just focused on the negative reports. They pointed out that even in the articles we didn't like, there were positive comments that we had not focused on. Generally speaking, our media want the same things we want for our children, and their support as well as their criticism serve our common purposes.

While you can hire the best communications director around, you can receive quality training, and you can practice beforehand, ultimately, the most important thing you can do is be forthright in your communications. We have emphasized that the public has a right to know and that public records are just that—public. We will work with the media at every opportunity, even at those times when we suspect that a situation may be a set-up. There is always an opportunity to reinforce your supporters' beliefs in the school system and to win over new supporters.

Your Communication Infrastructure

Going as an individual to speak before community groups and the media is one responsibility of the leader, one that requires a considerable investment of the leader's time and energy. Another, possibly even more important responsibility of the leader is to ensure that an infrastructure of varied communication vehicles is in place to support and advance your message. It is this infrastructure that will consistently deliver your message even in your absence. When the times are good and your audience is appreciative, communicating your message can be enjoyable and you will want to deliver your message by as many channels as possible (e.g., cable TV, newspaper, brochures, Web site, etc.). When times are not so good or your audience is less receptive to your message, there is another brand of courage required—this being the courage to speak the truth and accept the responsibilities.

In addition to the information that you share in first-person engagements, another tool in your communication infrastructure is the annual report that portrays pertinent information about the school district: test scores, SAT results, attendance, graduation rate, postsecondary education participation rates, teacher mobility, teacher certification, teacher and principal levels of education, facility information, existing and new programs, needs for technology and equipment, etc. The annual report should also show how your district compares locally, statewide, and nationally, and include both the good news and the bad. This report gives the leader an opportunity to craft the district's message and summarize results. You can highlight the district's mission and goals, and gauge achievement toward accomplishing them. Staffing challenges, trends, and other needs can be reviewed. Include survey results from parents, teachers, and students along with the interpretation of those data to provide a barometer on the district's health. Budget and finance information can be made available and understandable.

The annual report can also report on ways the leadership has attempted to engage the community, which will reveal much about your own personal leadership style. Complementing the annual report, timely newsletters can be distributed updating the significant events in the school district and highlighting some of the key programs and personnel. Web sites and cable TV must also be a part of your communication infrastructure.

The Importance of Your Web Site

A quality Web site is a must. It should be dynamic with current information updated regularly. Policies and procedures should be easily located on the Web site along with information on a myriad of topics of interest such as student assignment, curriculum objectives, facilities, awards, human resource assets, and a host of topical information. Internet links to individual schools should also be posted on the Web site making it a valuable information tool for the public.

There was a time when we didn't put a great deal of stock in Web sites. No longer. Your Web site is your main portal to the school district. An informative and user-friendly Web site that is updated constantly is one of the greatest PR tools you can have. With good factual information, you can get thousands of hits a day. We emphasize that the information has to be timely, well written, and leave the reader wanting more information. When, in 2003, WCPSS finally invested in a webmaster, we never regretted the decision. Put this expense in your budget. It will be well worth it.

Hire a skilled technician who strongly believes in continually improving the Web site.

Online feedback should be another important feature of your Web site. The Web site is a great tool for gathering information from the public, whether through survey format or just counting the number of hits on a particular topic. For example, we put questions on our Web site relative to student assignment issues. We asked parents if they were satisfied or if they were interested in appealing their child's placement to the board of education. We received feedback that gave us a feel for how many would be filing for an appeal.

If you're in administration, monitor your own Web site. Go to the site once a week and see what's there. Is the information timely? Are you thrilled with what you see there? Can it be navigated easily? The Web site must be user-friendly and provide useful information. For instance, the WCPSS Web site allows parents to enter their zip code or address and it will give them their child's school assignment and even their bus route. The Web site must give your consumers good, factual information that they can use and appreciate.

Using Video and Cable TV

Another tool in your communication infrastructure is video. A video program (live is great) can highlight students, teachers, and programs, providing information that is not normally available through the news media. Typically, the news media look for stories or events deemed newsworthy. The positive stories that you want to get before the public's attention are often buried in the back pages of the newspaper or scheduled for early Sunday morning TV; meanwhile, the negative stories will be on the front page or the lead story on the evening local news. Thus, the school district is responsible for highlighting positive events—success stories about students, schools, personnel, programs, facilities, and funding. Along with students and staff, the work of the school board, advisory councils, and PTAs can be featured on the cable program.

Cable channels are a little different than commercial networks. They see themselves as providing a service and not seeking an exposé. Cable channels look for programming opportunities. If you package your program appropriately, they will air it free of charge.

We take advantage of cable broadcasts and currently tape a half-hour show each week, in which we choose the topic, the school, and/or the people. For example, when we did a show on our magnet schools, we featured two teachers and the director of the district's magnet schools program. We discussed what magnet schools are, their programs, and how they operate.

We produce the cable show, edit it, and provide the tape to the cable services. We have learned that you can't just run out with a camcorder and tape the show. Have a plan—maybe even a script or at least a guideline. For each show, we had identified an individual whose job was to be the moderator and the communications department produced the show. We have been surprised to learn how many people view our cable shows, and it's amazing and gratifying to receive the many positive comments on something we have just shown. And by the way, you can also put the show on your Web site, produce CDs for later distribution, and use the tapes at civic group meetings.

When the decision was made to cablecast board meetings, we wanted people to act naturally while also remembering that the microphone is on and how important it was to be careful about "throw away" comments. Although you may worry that board members could use the cablecast as a bully pulpit, monopolizing time to make their point or plea to their constituency, we have seen that this is not a major problem. Rather, cable casting the board meetings is a great opportunity to allow the public to see what we are about—the problems we face and our decision-making process—as well as a way to publicly praise outstanding people within the district. An added plus is that with cable casting, we have a visual record and the opportunity to review tape for comments, facial expressions, gestures, body language, and the like.

Reaching Out

Your communication infrastructure should be all inclusive and should serve a dual purpose—first to get your message out, and second, to involve the community in decision-making processes.

Among many community groups, the faith community is an obvious place to conduct outreach and seek input. Do your homework by finding out the religious groups and organizations in your community and identify contact persons. We have found that all factions (Christian, Judaism, Muslim, or any other) have a desire to work with you to help children succeed academically. You only need to find the time and place for meeting. This could be Sunday or Saturday evening or any other time. We found one of the most satisfying events was to ask for a two-hour forum held in the evening. This was time for the superintendent to talk and to listen. Questions were encouraged and total honesty was the rule for everyone.

Like the media events, it is important to also prepare for these forums. For instance, if you are holding a forum sponsored by the Jewish Federation, anticipate that there will be questions related to Jewish holidays and where they appear in the calendar. And, while they may not be stated overtly, there will be questions asking whether the school district or school is proselytizing a particular religion.

In any religious community, there are some key figures that you can network with, and such connections will provide you with assistance when you encounter problems for which you may not know the answer or need help. When our district was dealing with the issues of 9–11 and al-Qaeda, we invited Muslim leaders into the schools to meet with principals and share ways our school leaders could be literate in supporting Muslim students and some of the issues they faced at that particular time.

While you want to take the message of the school district to diverse groups, religious and otherwise, remember that it is extremely important that the same message is delivered to all groups. Meeting with different groups is not about spinning your message to suit the interests of each group, but about making sure that the message is consistent and truthful.

Along with the faith-based community, other community groups for outreach are civic and social groups. Civic and social groups represented by the Kiwanis, Rotary, and Sertoma clubs, fraternities and sororities, and many other groups will all welcome interaction with the district leadership and usually have a service component as a part of their mission. Still other groups organize around particular issues such as problems confronting African American children, Latino and Hispanic children, poor children, or those receiving special education—all are elements of the community and will surely become detractors if not listened to and brought into the mainstream.

When speaking before community groups, there is always the question of how much information you should share. We believe you should share as much information as possible—the good, the bad, and the ugly. If it is controversial, you share it openly and honestly. Get the community's take on the issue and use that feedback to resolve it. Explain the district's position. Explain why the district has taken the position, share the complexities but not in a defensive way—then seek better solutions from the group. Be prepared because their solutions may not match yours and you must decide what to accept and what to reject. Regardless, explain fully your rationale for the position taken. Some will still disagree but you will gain respect for providing the forum.

A caution is necessary. Do not make policy based on meeting with only one group. This bears repeating. *Do not make policy based on a meeting with only one group,* because this represents only one voice for that issue. As a school leader, you must hear all the voices before formulating policy. Subsequently, when a policy is drafted, you may ask for feedback from various groups. While the policy is in draft form, collecting community feedback helps to create a policy that has community involvement, which usually leads to buy-in.

The Community Buys In

A perfect example of using communication processes to gain community buy-in happened for us when our district began its character education program. We invited every major religious group in the area to a school/community meeting on the topic. Approximately thirty to thirty-five people attended, representing most of the religious factions in the community. And there were individuals attending who were very vocal, even though it was not clear whose voice they represented. Of this mixed group, the question was asked, "If we are establishing a character education program, what/whose character traits should be included?" We recorded the feedback. The first round of sharing produced sixty-four traits that were recorded on chart paper and displayed on the wall. After more discussion, the list was condensed to thirty-two. From thirty-two, we were able to agree on sixteen, and from this sixteen, we finally settled on eight. Those eight character traits received the ownership of everyone at the table. Consequently, those eight character traits are still widely accepted by the community today, fifteen years later. Please understand, it is not the particular set of eight traits that we wish to emphasize—each school district may identify a different set of traits for its character education program—but, rather, we are emphasizing the process by which we came up with our set of traits. By engaging the community in this process we better ensured that the district's character education program would be widely accepted and ultimately the success that it has become.

The school district's implementation of these eight character traits has subsequently led to national recognition in character education for the school district. The payoff of our bringing such diverse groups together was major articles in national publications and a chance for the community to feel good about its part in developing the program. Ultimately, these character traits have been integrated in the curriculum and throughout the culture of the school district, with an outcome being better behavior on the part of the students and consistent modeling of this behavior on the part of staff and parents.

Your communication strategy must allow for community involvement. Community involvement pays off. Unquestionably, it is time consuming and requires that considerable energy be spent in the community, not only during work hours but nights and weekends. However, by doing so, the district's reputation becomes one of being open and accessible, willing to listen even to dissenting voices.

Organizing Advisory Groups

In addition to meeting with diverse community groups for specific purposes, the proactive leader will also form ongoing advisory groups. If you are truly seeking involvement, select a diverse group of citizens from across the district, making certain that they represent students in all different subgroups: race, grade level, geographic area, ethnicity, socio-economic status, disabilities, etc. Be inclusive.

At least three advisory groups are recommended: parents, staff, and students. These advisory groups form a vehicle for feedback. And, go an extra step and invite the leadership of these groups to participate in monthly meetings with the school district's top-level administrators to share their thinking and to be part of the decision making.

Faith-based organizations, civic groups and social clubs, special interest nonprofit groups, advisory councils—these are all community entities that can advance your school district mission. In good times, these groups will complement and supplement your efforts. At other times, should trouble arise, these forged relationships will determine if you have a community up in arms or a community willing to give you the benefit of the doubt because they have been at the table with you gaining an understanding of what it is you do, and how and why you do it. They can echo the district's mission, goal, objectives, and strategies. They know the test results and understand the trend over the past few years. They understand facility needs and your efforts to upgrade them. They have knowledge about teachers and staffing.

Finally, always keep in mind that your entire staff are important members of your communications team. The district leadership should not be the sole source that shares school information chapter and verse. When the public is talking about the school district in the grocery store, your teachers that are shopping in the aisles should be in the loop and able to share the district's philosophy and data. Your employee newsletter should keep your employees as well informed as possible. Not only must you as the district leader be informed, but it is also your responsibility to make certain that your principals and teachers are up to speed on where the district is, the changes being made, where you are headed, when you anticipate getting there, and what it will cost.

In many cases, the public believes that the top leader spends time defending the system and that the truth comes from the other ambassadors—the staff members—especially teachers. So, make certain that all staff and faculty are well informed of what is happening in your district. More than any business, a public school system must rely on its employees to spread the message. While a public school system will never have the PR fiscal resources like a business, it does have highly educated and dedicated employees with the common interest of advancing the education of children and youth.

Carefully allocated, the money you spend on communications with your stakeholders and community will yield many returns, helping everyone to get aboard the ship of quality education for all and alignment toward school systems goals.

Brand Name Recognition

When considering the variety of tools in your communication infrastructure, don't forget how important it is that you communicate a single message about the school district. Toward this end, ask yourself if you are marketing a unitary image that the public will immediately associate with your school or school district. Does your district have an image—what we refer to earlier as brand name recognition—of quality?

In WCPSS, there had been a hodgepodge of images with different central office departments using different style letterheads on their stationary, with Web pages on the district's Internet Web site varying according to the tastes (or skills) of each individual uploading to the Web site, and with no single design for a logo that represented the district. With the arrival of our communications director, we set out to improve that situation and we now have a common style for our central office letterhead, individual school letterhead, and Internet Web pages. Our logo—one that we have used for many years—now has specified dimensions, colors, and guidelines for how it is to be properly used on envelopes, letterhead, brochures, and the like. While a logo may seem like a small thing to be concerned about, we want no stone unturned when we are communicating with our public. Having brand name recognition like any business can only help us to instill confidence in our message. We want the public to think of quality when thinking of WCPSS, and we understand that it is up to us to advance this message.

Communicating in Challenging Times

The ultimate measure of a man is not where he stands in moments of comfort, but where he stands at times of challenge and controversy.

—Martin Luther King Jr.

In recent years, the business community has had its share of scandal and fraud. Where there is money involved, there is the ever present potential for abuse. Obviously, this is not true for all businesses or all business people; most operate honestly. But rest assured, every business is at risk for misuse of money. And, so too is every school system.

How you handle the bad news is especially telling of your leadership style, whether a business leader or school leader. Communicating good news is fun. Everyone likes to be the bearer of good news. That's the easy stuff. However, perhaps nothing is harder about being an effective leader than when you have bad news to communicate. Many CEOs and superintendents have lost their jobs because of bad news, sometimes because of the way it was communicated. Should you stonewall and refuse to admit that there's a problem? Should you hide it as long as possible? Should you distance yourself from the problem? Should you take action by firing a number of people? All of these activities are done, especially in government and big organizations; however, these are typically defensive remedies and are not usually designed to address the problem. Measures like these are designed more to shift the blame than to correct the problem. As in business, in public education there can be no substitute for taking action to correct a problem when it becomes apparent. The transportation fraud that we uncovered in our school district is an example.

At the time we uncovered fraud in our transportation department, the school district had a single internal auditor. This individual had been in place for a number of years and was doing an exemplary job in the district, which at the time was operating with a $750 million annual budget. This individual had too much work for a district of our size, but we did not have an appreciation for how we were putting ourselves at risk. After all, we were all well intentioned; we all had the best interests of children at heart, did we not? As we would learn, we had no idea that a cancer had been growing in the district for a number of years.

In May 2004, the district's accounting office reviewed invoices and began to suspect that there could be a financial problem in the transportation department. Transportation personnel were questioned and one employee affirmed our suspicions. Subsequently, the internal auditor took a closer look and decided to conduct a full-scale audit. After multiple interviews and volumes of reviewed paperwork, this auditor reported that the school system may have been defrauded. His initial investigation determined that there was the possibility of fraud and collusion among several transportation department leaders, as well as a vendor chosen by the department. At that time, no one had any real knowledge of the scope of this fraud but we soon realized the fraud could be in the millions of dollars. Only the news media are excited to learn of news like that. Those with oversight of the transportation department and district leadership were astonished but determined to learn the truth and make things right.

Two years later, eight people were in jail for lengthy felony terms. The fraud had cost the district nearly $4 million, but almost $5 million was recovered in restitution and penalties. When all was said and done, the district had exacted justice, strengthened its system of internal controls, and weathered the bad news generated by the fraud. While our public rightfully held us accountable and rightfully demanded that no such event occur again, our response to the fraud did much to bolster the public's confidence. Evidence of this is that the superintendent's second in command at the time of the fraud is now superintendent of the district, in part, on the strength of how he and the district handled the fraud investigation and pledged to improve school district accountability. And, in November 2006, the public approved the largest school bond at the time in the nation for almost $1 billion to build new schools and upgrade technology. The approach we took to handling the fraud investigation was in no small measure responsible for regaining the public's confidence.

Obviously, the right thing to do was to conduct a complete and public investigation. Not only did our internal auditor turn his full attention to this matter, but we additionally reported our suspicions to the county commissioners, the county district attorney, the state attorney general's office—and the media. The next two years were very challenging, but trying to hide the investigation or give it some kind of spin would have been unwise. Rather, we decided to uncover the truth, make it known, and learn from it.

What we learned was amazing. Staff in the transportation department had colluded to spend taxpayers' dollars for personal items, including department store gift cards, televisions, home carpeting, a jet ski, and even a camping trailer. Fake invoices with one of the school district's larger parts' suppliers had been created and approved by the transportation department head. The individual invoices had been kept below $2,500 so as to not prompt a higher level of organizational scrutiny. This scheme required a number of individuals within the transportation department to work in concert to defraud the system. The scheme also required employees of the supplier to be involved with kick backs in cash and property. As we learned, the collusion had been going on for a period of several years and was growing in scope. Auditors will tell you that fraud is very difficult to detect and collusion among several parties is particularly challenging to uncover. However, greed seems to know no bounds and the wrongdoing unravels pretty quickly once it comes to light.

Once we had become suspicious, the posture the school district administration thereafter took was one of openness and thorough investigation; wherever the road led, we would deal with the problem. The internal auditor and a team consisting of the superintendent, the deputy superintendent, the assistant superintendent for human resources, and others dug deeper into this issue. As this team uncovered layers of fraud, information about the high-dollar purchases began to surface. As the team continued to probe, we started to get some idea of the magnitude of the problem. Our initial thought was that the fraud may involve one or two low-level people in transportation and perhaps a low-level vendor. However, we soon realized this was much bigger and we consulted with our school board's attorneys who became a part of the review team to help us to follow the money trail.

Key members of the team met at least three times weekly to review findings from the auditor and attorneys. We began to learn that more people were involved than originally thought and that the fraud appeared to extend higher in the transportation department than originally thought. Much to the superintendent's disappointment, the investigation led to a close personal friend and neighbor, someone he had known and trusted for thirty-seven years. This finding disappointed the superintendent professionally and personally; nevertheless, our determination to proceed was never in doubt. Full disclosure at all costs. Advise the board of education and bring them up to speed, and contact the district attorney to let him know a crime had evidently been committed.

We had moved with deliberate speed to clarify for ourselves our suspicions. Only two months elapsed from the point in time of first suspecting the fraud, collecting reams of information to verify this likelihood, and formally notifying the board of education.

The school board met in a special executive session, which signaled to the news media that something of import was being discussed. How would we share this information with the media? We readily decided that the information is public record and that we should have full disclosure to the extent permissible. We didn't convene a press conference, we just made ourselves available. Our behavior was to hide nothing; we knew the wisdom of the old adage that it's not the wrongdoing that will get you fired—it's the cover up.

After the district attorney was notified, he called in the State Bureau of Investigation (SBI). With the involvement of the SBI, a lead SBI investigator was named and the district provided access to all books, records, and personnel. We provided any assistance required, even to the extent of reserving rooms for investigators and news media to meet. We met with the editorial board of the local newspaper, spoke on camera with the video media, did a half-hour show on television, did radio clips, wrote a point of view column to the newspaper, sent a parent newsletter home, and encouraged senior staff to voluntarily ask for interviews with the SBI.

At the height of the fraud investigation, the superintendent was invited to appear on *Headline Saturday TV.* Remember everything we've discussed earlier in this chapter about dealing with the media? Well, here was a test if ever there was a test! Admittedly, this was Saturday and the show would be competing with football games for the public's attention. Even so, the name of the show alone could be enough to intimidate. We had to prepare and we did. We practiced and were ready when the first question out of the box was, "How could you not know of the fraud, given the amount of money that was involved?" That's the kind of question that could cause you to stammer, look away, and sweat. But we had anticipated the question. The communications director and the superintendent had practiced the question, as well as many variations of this and other questions, in the days before going on the TV show. We knew that question would come and we knew too that the media was probably misinformed. Yes, we had to answer why it was that we didn't know about the fraud—at least until the time that we caught it—and we were able to correct the media's misinformation. Knowing the tenor of the probable line of questioning, the superintendent was prepared to take his time answering the questions, knew that he didn't need to become defensive, and was able to watch for opportunities to correct misinformation.

When you go public and provide full disclosure as we did, doing so keeps the news story on the front burner. *Headline Saturday TV* would not be the end of the media's interests in this story.

What made this story especially interesting were the kinds of purchases made by the culprits. The more we learned, the more astonished we were—jet skis, big screen TVs, a beach camper, computers, gift cards, even a truck. According to the district attorney, the total approached $4 million, a figure he had arrived at by looking at all invoices written to the vendor. Interestingly, this figure somewhat misrepresented the extent of the fraud because some of the invoices had actually been legitimate; appropriate goods and services had been received. However, this was a point that we weren't going to argue. The size of the fraud was simply too big to be quibbling over which purchases were fraudulent and which were not.

Leaders need to understand that they will face considerable stress and scrutiny in situations like ours with the intense media coverage. An expected response among leaders might be for each to look for cover, to assign blame to others, and find those sacrificial lambs that could be terminated. "If person XYZ had been doing his or her job better, this never would have happened!" But fraud does happen; where there is money, there is the potential for abuse. As we became more informed about fraud, we learned that some research suggests only 6 percent of fraud is caught and the average time of a fraudulent event may extend over four years.

We understood that the blame game—finding, in effect, innocent scapegoats—would be counterproductive. Rather than seeking two or three such individuals that we could blame for poor leadership, we elected to work together, which meant that we were committed to identifying the extent of the problem, getting the public's money back, and sending the culprits to jail. We were after answers, not blame. We wanted to come out of the investigation stronger and better able to prevent future instances of fraud.

When the investigation was completed, the district attorney found that the fraud had not gone any higher than the transportation department. The school district recovered a little over $4 million from the supplier, goods that had been seized were auctioned off bringing another $500,000, and the criminals repaid money to the district. Following the investigation, the school board hired a forensics audit firm to conduct a districtwide investigation of other potential weaknesses in internal controls and opportunities for fraudulent behavior. This firm's report found that the district was well managed. In record time, the county commissioners supported us based on the findings and recommendations of the forensic audit as did the state auditors. Suggestions were made in the forensic audit and many new control measures are now in place.

Of course, one of the very first corrections we made was to increase the staffing of the internal auditor's office. Like most school districts trying to be a good steward of the public's money, we work to keep the central office administrative staffing low. You want most of your people working in the schools with children. But, sometimes you can be penny-wise and pound-foolish. One major lesson we learned was that cutting auditing costs for the sake of more classroom dollars has its limits. An internal audit department must be properly staffed and, complementing the internal audit function, a citizens' audit committee can be very helpful in restoring public confidence.

In 2005, the school district established a citizens' audit committee—the first of its kind in the state. Another change the district has made is to embed finance administrators in all the major departments; these individuals report to the accounting department but also support departmental administrators with managing their budgets. A word to the wise—school board member, superintendent, or principal—you can cut costs only so much beyond which you place yourself at risk for mismanagement.

The story of the transportation fraud is not over and the new superintendent has made expanding fiscal accountability one of his four strategic directives for leadership. Still, much of the fraud event is now behind the district. We had had our trial by fire and did the right thing; for this, we earned the community's respect. And, like the community, we are especially pleased that the criminals are in jail.

To speak of courage! In WCPSS, there had been no previous experience with fraud of this nature and magnitude. Facing the issue squarely and resolving the issue with integrity required the courage of a great many individuals, both within and outside the school system. The district's communication infrastructure was tasked and found up to the challenge.

Whatever size school district you have, know that the value you place on communication, the varied means by which you communicate, and the audiences with which you communicate all contribute to your success.

WHAT YOU CAN DO TO IMPROVE

- Understand that communications with your public create new opportunities for improvement
- Seek the help of local marketing and public relations executives
- Appreciate that communications with your own employees are instrumental to goal alignment and school district success
- Accept that you will need to spend some money—do so wisely and get the most from targeted communications
- Go public with the bad news—hesitate and you will lose the momentum to make things better
- Adequately budget for your own internal audit processes

BUSINESS PARTNERSHIPS THAT MAKE A DIFFERENCE

Business and education leaders have tended to look at each other with suspicion across a chasm of seemingly different leadership styles, purposes, regulations, etc. However, it is our premise that there are more similarities than there are differences between business and education and, without question, we need each other. What would business be without highly educated employees and what would public education be without the advocacy of business? It is necessary to develop better ways and means for these two forces in our society to find the common ground where we can meet and support each other.

The Concept and Formation of BELC

The report *A Nation at Risk*, published in 1983, highlighted the mediocrity of our public schools and was a wake-up call for school reform. School reform efforts that followed in the wake of that report took many different approaches, one of which was the Secretary's Commission on Achieving Necessary Skills (SCANS).[10] Initiated by the former Secretary of Labor, Lynn Martin, SCANS provided American business a means of communicating with educators about the competencies and skills that students needed to be successful in the workplace. Reform efforts deriving from SCANS were designed to look at the whole issue of teaching and learning in the context of applied skills. Were the lessons we were teaching in the classroom of the nature that students could subsequently apply what they were learning successfully in the world of work? For instance, the SCANS report emphasized that appropriate contexts for learning should be designed to

- Require the integration of knowledge, procedures, and their application
- Engage the sense-making efforts of the student
- Require active construction and invention
- Engage multiple skills of different types and require students to integrate these in a performance
- Include the social interactions and resources and tools typical of nonschool situations

As we entered the 1990s, educators began to talk about preparing students for the skills of the twenty-first century. If we in public education were to become competent helping our students develop these workplace skills, it was clear that we needed a better understanding of how these skills could be taught through the curriculum. We began to appreciate that this understanding could only be crystallized through a strong network of business partners, and we realized that we needed to bring businesses under our umbrella as partners in education to prepare young people to be successful after they left public education. Accordingly, we went looking for business partners and promised our prospective partners that we would update our knowledge to stay current with the latest business practices, and based on this, would change how we taught students. From these early beginnings, we formed a group that we called the Business Education Leadership Council (BELC). Through BELC, we planned to bring businesses into a partnership with public education.

For many years, schools have looked at businesses as a source of funds and resources. Businesses are used to being asked for all kinds of "things," but are not often asked for their expertise. Because we knew that educators and businesses would need to work closely together in these new times, in BELC we wanted a relationship rather than a handout. We wanted to involve businesses in all aspects of our educational program.

BELC began in 1993 and today remains a unique example in this country for involving businesses in the education of children. In the fifteen years since, BELC has changed for the better how Wake County's schools partner with businesses to improve education.

In the early 1990s, forerunners to BELC had already begun to organize in different forms in areas of the county. Each took a slightly unique approach to the same question—how can local business people have a positive impact on public high school education other than by donating money? From these beginnings, the structure of BELC began to take shape with help from then Associate Superintendent McNeal, key district administrators, principals, and business leaders. During the mid-1990s, the BELC model was refined and replicated across the county. Once McNeal became superintendent in 2000, he insisted that his principals write their business alliance into their annual school improvement plan, giving the alliance the weight it needs to ensure its continuity. Now, at every high school and middle school in Wake County, there are business alliance partners.

School administrators from across the country and internationally have come to Wake County wanting to know how we organized and continue to sustain BELC. What these visitors find to be especially amazing is that there is no budget for BELC other than two school district staff members who keep things organized across the county. BELC impacts thousands of students in a way that teachers cannot for the mere cost of two employees in a 134,000 student school district—now that is a business partnership that makes a difference!

Where BELC Is Today

Even as our district continues to grow, we have been successful in our efforts to continue forming business alliances in all of our high schools and middle schools. After an organizational meeting at the outset of the school year, at each school a group of about ten business people meet monthly with the school principal and designated staff members to plan and carry out projects designed to help all students understand why they need a good high school education. In these meetings, staff will talk about the school and student needs vis-à-vis a particular business initiative. For example, a printing business might help the school with some of the flyers that the school wants to distribute or provide some afterschool work for students to help produce the flyers. This printing business will also help the teachers and students know what skills are necessary to be successful in the printing business. How well must students be able to read and write and handle math to be successful in the printing business? How much business acumen do you need if you're doing inventory, ordering supplies, or marketing your product? What recourse do you have if you find that you're operating at a loss? Where can you go to get a loan? What about interest rates? Even, how do you start a business? Lessons also extend to the business environment where the student can see the printing business in action.

Over the school year, many of the district's school-business relationships play out in one-to-one relations with an individual teacher or student interacting directly with an individual business person, and the most important aspect of this relationship is how entire systems are impacted. For instance, one business alliance between a teacher and business person may open the door for students to intern, job shadow, be mentored, and perhaps even be hired by the business. Having a close relationship with business professionals, our teachers also benefit through being appraised of the changing dynamics in the business world. And, of course, our business leaders have a much greater opportunity to learn about our schools and students, as well as our needs and how to be active supporters of public education.

At the end of the year, school administrators and business members tally up how many students and teachers have been positively impacted. When these numbers are collected for the entire school district, thousands of students have been directly impacted.

Presently, we estimate that the school district has at least 400 businesses participating in BELC. The group that is responsible for guiding this effort districtwide is the school district's Career and Technical Education (CTE) office. Staff in this office seek out new partnerships (as do teachers and administrators in the schools), monitor the development of these new partnerships, facilitate communications throughout BELC, and host recognition ceremonies honoring business partners and schools. When a business signs up with BELC, it is connected with the CTE staff as well as other business members who together help the "newbie" establish itself with its school and the BELC organization.

What Works and What Doesn't

One of the first things we realized when working with businesses is that there may be some reluctance to work with our schools and school staff. Potential business partners sometimes fear that all we want is their money and that we have very little interest in their expertise. We found that prospective business partners had to be convinced that we were serious about listening to them, along with training our teachers to work with business leaders and making adjustments to our curriculum based on their input. Accordingly, the school district administration emphasized with our school principals and their staff how important it was that the schools not simply ask for money, but instead seek to build longer, more meaningful relations in which learning is the goal of the partnerships—schools learning about businesses and businesses learning about schools. In fact, the businesses often do provide resources that have monetary value but we do not allow this to become the main reason for the relationship.

We have also learned that building the business relationship is not done overnight. A strong relationship takes years to build and this relationship has to be worked on every day. It's similar to marriage. The key to every school-business partnership is communication. There are monthly meetings throughout the year and one of the main purposes of these meetings is to make sure that everyone's questions—ours and theirs—are answered. In the course of these communications, it is important to distinguish between practices, skills, and knowledge that transfer well between schools and businesses and those that do not. Although we emphasize in this book the value of using business practices in our schools, we also know that we cannot expect to run a school exactly like a business.

Benefits BELC Has Brought to Schools

Having started BELC in the early to mid-1990s, we have now established a network of businesses that are advocates for public education. We know that we can count on the business community for tremendous support. The best example of how this has made a difference for us is the support that the business community gave the school district when the $970 million dollar bond referendum was put on the ballot before the community in 2006. Passing this bond would require a tax increase and the critics fought hard to defeat the referendum. In the end, the critics were over-matched—we had business on our side.

Other examples of benefits we have realized through BELC is the Greater Raleigh Chamber of Commerce Web site where students can describe a business interest and be connected to appropriate people in the business community. Previously in this book, we have discussed the citizen's advisory councils; many members of these councils come from the business community, in many instances with BELC backgrounds. And, the financial experts the superintendent brought in to oversee the budget for the district come from the business community, often again with BELC experience.

Conversely, our business partners have realized benefits as well. Without question, the involvement of businesses in our schools is contributing to a strong economy; with the help of our business community, we are producing students better prepared for post-secondary pursuits, whether continuing their education or entering the world of work. Although it is difficult to quantify, probably the greatest benefit our business partners realize is in "giving back." Each of us in education and business can probably point to one or more teachers who helped advance our career aspirations, and giving back to the next generation can be a very satisfying experience.

WHAT YOU CAN DO TO IMPROVE

- Bring business leaders into your decision-making processes
- Emphasize that you are seeking advice, consultation, and expertise rather than financial contributions
- Help open doors for your school principals to meet and connect with the business community
- Establish a "Business Alliance" with the mission to match individual businesses to individual schools, beginning with the high schools then the middle schools

NOTES

1. Having said this, we too are familiar with the business scandals that have been prominent in the news in recent years. When we speak of businesses and business leaders, we mean the many exemplary models that we find in our own neighborhoods and communities.

2. To us, a stretch goal is more than simply setting one's sights high. Additionally, a stretch goal requires that educators and community members alike appreciate that continuing to do "business as usual" will not suffice.

3. We need to mention a major difference between WCPSS and many other national school systems. In North Carolina, school district boards of education have no ability to raise revenue from taxes. That power lies with the state legislature and the county commissioners.

4. Data for the years 1998 through 2003 are found in a report produced by the school district's Evaluation and Research Department, E&R Report No. 04.28. (Wake County Public School System. [2004]. *Measuring Up*. Retrieved October 27, 2007, from http://www.wcpss.net/evaluation-research/reports/2004/0428outcomes03_04.pdf) Data for the years 1994 through 1997 are organized from a variety of WCPSS sources.

5. Extolling the virtues of openness, Thomas Friedman, in his book *The Lexus and the Olive Tree*, makes the point that "the culture you create around secrecy is a slower culture suited to a slower world. As a company you always end up overvaluing what you know and undervaluing what is out there in plain sight" (Anchor Books, 2000, p. 226).

6. Between the 1985–86 and 2007–08 school years, WCPSS enrollment more than doubled, growing from 57,268 to 134,002, and projections are that this growth will continue well into the future.

7. We are fortunate in our school district to have the support of the Wake Education Partnership. WEP is a community-based public education advocacy organization, but is not a mouthpiece for the school district. WEP does not hesitate to offer up well-deserved criticisms.

8. Following the unexpected death of Robert McGehee, CEO of Progress Energy, in October 2007, within a week the board of directors had named William Johnson to be his successor. Previously, Johnson had been the chief operating officer. Compare the efficiency of this succession planning to that of most school boards that often take months to identify a successor.

9. In many situations around the country, there is often talk about hiring a business person for the superintendency. We certainly don't rule out this possibility; however, it is necessary to take the full measure of the person including the individual's value system. Our experience in public education suggests caution is warranted. The superintendent's job is to lead principals and teachers; these individuals must have confidence in their superintendent's bottom line, which, for the dedicated educator, is providing the highest quality education for every child. Should a business person not hold this value in his or her heart, but instead see the bottom line as a matter of dollars and cents, then education could suffer at the "expense" of business efficiencies or cost-cutting measures. Hire an educator for your superintendent and a business person for your chief financial officer.

10. Kane, M., Berryman, S., Goslin, D., & Meltzer, A. (1990). *The secretary's commission on achieving necessary skills: Identifying and describing the skills required by work*. Washington, DC: Pelavin Associates, Inc. Retrieved February 17, 2007, from http://wdr.doleta.gov/SCANS/idsrw/idsrw.pdf

Leadership and Brains

Now lookit, Dorothy, you ain't using your head about Miss Gulch.
Think you didn't have any brains at all. . . . When you come home,
don't go by Miss Gulch's place. Then Toto won't get in her garden,
and you won't get in no trouble . . . your head ain't made of straw,
you know.

—Hunk in *The Wizard of Oz*

Brains demonstrate the capacity to continuously improve, resulting in lifelong learning. In education, we seek to create a culture of excellence, which requires brains along with courage and heart. For us, using our brains has a lot to do with how we plan and how we use data. For years we have studied the Baldrige National Quality program, Total Quality Management, and the Plan/Do/Study/Act cycle described by W. Edwards Deming, and we have appreciated the importance of planning and use of data.

If brains are essential (who will argue?), then, how do you help brains develop? One answer is to develop your own in-house training program. If you do this, the uniqueness of your organization requires that you not adopt a "one-size-fits-all" approach to training. For instance, contrast an in-house training program that allows you to tailor curriculum and instructional modules to specific needs of your district, to a university course of study in which the curriculum hasn't had a significant revision in many years. Don't get us wrong—we recognize the university course of study has its place—however, we also believe that school districts need to develop their own brainpower as well.

Even staff meetings and retreats should be seen as opportunities to develop our brains, building on a continuous theme of excellence. It is important to set high goals that will be owned by the organization with all stakeholders participating in the goal-setting process. Similarly, using our brains, we also know that all evaluations, objectives, strategies, and budgets should be aligned to the district's goals. And, all communication should be focused on how successful we are in our efforts to be excellent. Planning, using data, developing in-house talent, and aligning major initiatives are all examples of using our brains.

This section is the most business-like of our book. Business people will see these chapters as the building blocks of corporate success: goal setting, planning, training, metrics for success, and saving money. All of these processes and activities apply equally well to education and must be done effectively to achieve excellence.

GOAL SETTING AND PLANNING

Everyone has goals—sometimes big goals, sometimes little goals—but always something toward which we are striving. In an organization, whether a business or a school district, there will be individuals with personal goals and there will also be the goals of the organization. How well the personal and organization goals fit together will be a significant aspect of how well the organization functions, and the process by which an organization sets it goal(s) may be a harbinger of future success. For instance, will it be only the top leadership that sets the organizational goal(s) or will everyone be involved? Will only organization members participate in the goal setting or will the consumers or surrounding community have involvement? Who are the key stakeholders in goal setting and how are they involved? And, what manner and forms of planning will be needed, both in setting the goal and seeing it through?

Goal Setting

You have read how the Goal 2003 experience changed education in Wake County for the better. Our plans for Goal 2003 very nearly came true; we made significant progress toward achieving the goal of having 95 percent of our third- and eighth-grade students proficient in reading and mathematics. In 2002, after years of great success, the school board wisely thought we should take the next step—Goal 2008. We had made significant progress with Goal 2003 and we now needed to determine how to build upon that progress.

Having learned how to effectively involve the community, during the process of developing Goal 2008 we held many meetings with stakeholders—parents, teachers, business leaders, faith community, and elected officials. We wanted to establish the right goal and to ensure there was a consensus that the new goal was the best for the district. The goal we developed was as follows: *WCPSS is committed to academic excellence. By 2008, 95 percent of students in Grades 3 through 12 will be at or above grade level as measured by the State of North Carolina End-of-Grade or Course tests, and all student groups will demonstrate high growth.* Additionally, we identified a number of strategies to deploy in pursuit of this goal.

- Increase challenging educational opportunities for all students
- Increase student participation and success in advanced classes at the high school level
- Increase the percent of ninth-grade students graduating from high school within four years
- Recruit, develop, support, and retain a highly qualified workforce to ensure student success
- Identify and seek resources necessary to support student success
- Build a consensus of support through community collaboration

Everyone loved it. It was taking the next step, building on the success of Goal 2003 by adding high school students to the mix. Everything had been done right; all stakeholders were involved in establishing Goal 2008. Now, almost five years later, what has been our progress? Unfortunately, the progress has not been as dramatic as it was with Goal 2003. In fact, some might question if we've made any progress. When we ask ourselves, how this could be, we have had to face some tough answers. Our planning may not have been adequate and/or subsequent events may have necessitated changes to our plans.

Looking back, one lesson we now understand is that we had taken an educator's approach to the challenge of setting our next goal but we did not fully appreciate the business end of getting the goal done. A major oversight is that we had forgotten about the monetary cost of achieving success. Goal 2003 had been largely achieved without additional state or local funding by realigning school programs and spending to target the results we wanted. While that was good business practice in one regard—getting the most out of existing resources—in another regard, we failed to understand that the progress we made toward Goal 2003 did in fact come with a monetary cost, and the district had few resources left to "realign" or "reallocate" for the difficult task of Goal 2008.

We can also say that we have learned we didn't fully understand that the significant challenges we would face at the high school level would be very different from those we faced at the elementary and middle grades. We found implementing change at the high school to be more difficult for reasons such as there being more specialization of courses and more personal investment in this specialization; schedule changes have greater impact on both staff and students (e.g., cocurricular and extracurricular activities, availability of facilities); and the sheer number of students can hinder staff ability to build personal relationships at the high school level.

Additionally, other factors that were difficult to forecast in our planning and out of our control also impacted Goal 2008. Growth in student enrollment that had been occurring since the mid-1980s began to accelerate dramatically after 2000, further stretching resources. On top of challenges faced by growth, our state Department of Public Instruction changed one of the major metrics for measuring success. In the 2005–06 year, the state raised the bar for satisfactory performance in elementary and middle grade mathematics. Where once we had 80–90 percent of third- through eighth-grade students achieving at or above grade level in math, after the bar was raised for mathematics in 2005–06, now we fell back by 5–10 percentage points at each grade level.

While the new Goal 2008 was widely praised, we overreached, in part due to not understanding that the goal was underfunded, in part due to not forecasting how the district might be impacted by growth, and in part due to not even thinking of the possibility of changing metrics. Our planning had not gotten us to where we wanted to be. Still, not all was lost. It is said that hindsight is twenty-twenty; things become very clear when we look back. And, it is also true that what you learn from your shortcomings in planning makes you stronger when you plan for the next round.

All things considered, our failure to secure the needed funding was probably the biggest barrier to achieving Goal 2008. The state will not give additional funding to an affluent school system at the expense of another. And, school leaders had not asked the county if they were interested in additional success to the point of spending more money on it. Our failure to seek and secure the needed funding is probably the critical mistake.

We had adopted a major goal and promoted it without planning for the needed funds to get it done. We spent a lot of time on community involvement and word-smithing, but we forgot some obvious questions: How much will it cost to achieve? Were the county commissioners willing to pay for it? What we should have done was to take our Goal 2003 success right to the county leadership and determine first if these leaders would be willing to take it to the next level, including what it would cost, how it would be measured, and what the benefits would be—then involve them in the community process so that the goal would become their goal as much as the community goal. With the involvement of the commissioners in developing community support, it would be more palatable for the commissioners to propose raising taxes to increase the needed funding for this landmark goal. Unfortunately, we didn't follow this process. Hopefully, we will with our next goal.

Involvement of Community in Planning

One of the facets of a successful school district is its ability to deal with diverse opinions and critics. Frequently, the criticism is related to lack of information, poor communication, and an agenda that may be counter to where the school district needs to head. The challenge is convincing the community that their agenda is your agenda, with everyone coming into alignment and moving in the same direction.

As we looked at the success of Goal 2003, we admitted we were unsuccessful in our efforts to achieve our goal for 95 percent of students at or above grade level, including all subgroups. However, we did achieve a composite score of almost 92 percent with no major subgroup below 78 percent. We shared all of the numbers and corresponding data with the community. We did so by sending flyers home, re-establishing our speakers' bureau, etc. We showed the community the significant progress we had made with Goal 2003 and gave credit to all the partners who helped us. We thanked our teachers, our principals, the commissioners, the school board, the faith community, the business community, and of course our students. All of these elements were integral in the success that we achieved with Goal 2003.

Working with the PTA Council leadership, we had developed a plan to bring in 3,000 volunteers to help us reach Goal 2003. In fact, we enlisted more than 20,000 volunteers over the period of working toward Goal 2003. We were shocked that so many people were willing to volunteer, although in retrospect we shouldn't have been surprised. Divided by 120 schools, the 20,000 volunteers works out to be an average of about 170 volunteers per school. Now, there is a public relations force! If these 20,000 volunteers talk to two others about the good things happening in our schools, that's 60,000 who can be supporters for the district. We have reaped the rewards of this volunteer group in the areas of budget support, conversion to year-round schools, re-election of board members, and the emergence of the school district as a national success story.

After all of this celebration and back slapping about our success with Goal 2003, school district leaders came to a Wake Education Partnership (WEP) summit, shared all this information, and said that we had unfinished business. Here was the beginning of Goal 2008. WEP published a report called *Quality Matters*—their independent review of our district—in which they praised the success of Goal 2003 and supported the idea of Goal 2008. We re-emphasized with the community that we wanted 95 percent of all our students at grade level, and then we ratcheted up the challenge. We wanted to be at 95 percent with all groups experiencing high growth. We told the community that we needed the same dedication and more with Goal 2008.

Board of Education—Getting on Board

Re-election weighs heavily on the minds of board of education members. Most want to know where they sit with their constituency. Many board members create their own information sessions to keep parents in their districts informed. Frequently, staff are invited to make presentations. These forums provided us opportunities to show how much progress we were making under the two goals—the narrowing of the achievement gap, the progress of majority students, and the rise in SAT and AP scores. Board members were able to use this information to make the case that everything the board does is designed to achieve the goal of academic excellence for all students—even when dealing with the touchy issue of student reassignment or conversion of traditional schools to year-round schools. What better posture for board members to be in than one in which they can say they support the goal of 95 percent of their students at or above grade level?

Getting "on board" required constant study for board members. One issue that was time consuming was enrollment growth, and it continues to be so today. Board members learned the impact of overenrolled schools on achievement and facilities. For instance, with twenty mobile units on campus, students frequently wait in lines to use the bathroom, water fountain, and even the media center, and much instructional time is lost. Safety issues are posed with isolated children walking from the mobile units into the school to use the bathroom. If we couldn't keep all of our schools diverse, healthy, and not crowded, what impact would this have on teacher, parent, and student outcomes? The process of planning for Goals 2003 and 2008 contributed significantly to the education of both established and new board members, so much so that it begged the question of whether we could plan even further ahead.

Vision 2020

The significant impact of population growth throughout our community affected every single classroom in Wake County and we have been heavily criticized. "How did you let this happen?" "Why didn't we have a plan to build more schools to keep up with the growth?" "Why couldn't we project the numbers more accurately?" Never mind that our state's Department of Transportation hasn't been able to build highways fast enough, or that the housing community cannot keep up with supply and demand, or that the water and sewer systems are overwhelmed. Regardless, our critics said that if we had a long-range plan we wouldn't have been blindsided by this unprecedented growth.

Vision 2020 was an attempt by school and community leaders to take a fifteen-year look at growth in the community, realizing that the farther out you look, the less reliable your model will be. Still, we could make a prediction based on growth numbers, live births, immigration, graduation rates, retention rates, dropouts, and mobility in and out of the county. Using these variables, we came up with a projected number of students through the year 2020 and calculated how much more classroom space we would need, ultimately including the number of new schools needed. We created all of this information working directly with municipalities, real estate developers, and consultants at North Carolina State University. Thus was born Vision 2020, listing how many schools we would need for the next fifteen years; where we needed these schools; what schools would need renovation given their age; and the ultimate cost of this vision: all in response to what some in the community said was our lack of long-range planning. Although only a few years have passed since we first developed Vision 2020, it is already apparent that results from this effort will be mixed. We still have to run the numbers every year because variables can and do change, and it has not changed our need to make adjustments every year.

The critics who advocated for Vision 2020 did so thinking that a long-range plan would eliminate the need to reassign students every year. However, we lack a funding mechanism that will bring a regular flow of capital dollars to our district that would allow us to add new schools as needed. When you are always playing catch up with building new schools, and new schools are overcrowded from the day they open, reassignment will be necessary for some time to come.

What we have learned from Vision 2020, we should have learned long ago. In many situations when we are criticized, we respond with a study or task force. If we plan for it ourselves and appoint the committee members ourselves, the results are invariably criticized. Strangely enough, Vision

2020 was criticized as planning for way too much growth. Critics said that the motive behind this planning was simply to get more schools from bond money. In fact, the initial projections made in Vision 2020 are now proving to have been too low. Have the critics been silenced? No, now the criticism is that the planning effort was wasting money, reminding us of Rodney Dangerfield's phrase, "I don't get no respect."

Regardless, we know that through planning we can improve our own practices, and we have also learned the value of including diverse parties and perspectives in any planning effort, study, or task group. Here, we can say there is a major difference in the parallels that we have been developing with business practices insofar as businesses tend to not spend a lot of time and money trying to win the support of a group that has always been in opposition. Instead, a business will probably focus on getting more support from their existing supporters who in turn can help the business win new customers. Unlike business, however, in education, we should make no claims that we have cornered the market on excellence; rather, we are always striving to improve and we need to be open to the ideas of even our detractors.

WHAT YOU CAN DO TO IMPROVE

- Set goals, but not so many that you can't monitor the progress you are making toward them all

- Include those within and outside your system that control funding streams in the goal development process

- Include also the naysayers in the goal development process

- Make sure your board of education is committed to the process and outcomes

- Be careful to not look too far ahead—five years may be about as far out as you want to look—there are too many unknowns with long-term planning

- Be prepared to make mid-course adjustments when critical variables incorporated in your planning change

MAKING USE OF RETREATS

Sometimes it is helpful to get out of the office. A change of scenery and being away from the constant interruptions of the business or school office can help clear the head and allow for a more relaxed consideration of the "big picture." The staff retreat is commonly employed in both business and education and, when well organized and implemented, can make a significant contribution to the success of the organization.

Effective Board Retreats

Service on a school board is very challenging, whether it is a small school district with taxing authority or one with 100,000 students and no taxing authority. Much rides on the decisions of the school board, although not the education of the individual students—the teachers take care of that. Rather, the efficiency of operations depends heavily on a school board that does its own job and not the job of the administrators.

Many school board members have never served in large organizations like a business board with a competent staff. Many go through the pain of running for office to earn the position and gain the authority that comes with it. But once there, new board members may be unsure of what to do with the authority of the office. Some want to visit every school and meet every principal. Some want to review curriculum in great detail. Everyone wants to talk to the superintendent—sometimes every day. None of this would take place in a business of similar size.

Board retreats provide opportunities for board members to plan and develop consensus around the nature of their role and responsibilities. Most school board retreats are similar. Board members brainstorm democratically, develop ideas about where they want the school system to be in the future, and end up with a lot of issues and concerns in the "parking lot"—definitely a long-term parking lot, because demands on their time result in struggles to get back to many of the items. For board retreats to make any real progress, superintendents and their staff must help the board members learn to work well together.

In a public company, all of the board members typically have business experience. They are familiar with the challenges of running a business, even if it is in a different industry. They also know what their duties are and what they are not. And when they cross that line, the chair of the board brings them back into line. The best retreat any newly seated school board could have would be one run by a business consultant familiar with the ways of running a business board. A large part of the retreat should be learning how to work well together, using school board examples of past mistakes to prepare for the future. Some examples of basic things that have to be understood and agreed to are the following:

- The chair's job is to keep the board members working well together, not to run the daily operations of the school system.
- When a decision is final, it is the board's decision even if some voted against it.
- The chair speaks to the media for the board. The media usually want controversy to make stories interesting and they know that

controversy is easier to fabricate—or at least spin up—when each individual board member speaks to the media.

- On major issues like school bonds and budgets, the board should maintain a united front to the public—no matter how they voted as individuals. Lack of unanimity creates a lack of trust in the community, which leads directly to a lack of support.

At the start of any retreat, focus on helping board members work together. Then use the rest of the time to educate the board on important education issues at hand for the next twelve months and seek their input. Lastly, get their feedback on what the staff is doing right and wrong from the community's standpoint. After all, the purpose of the school board is to represent the community in guiding local education decisions.

School board service is said to be a thankless job. Whether or not the members find it thankless is debatable, but all find it very time consuming. Bear this in mind when you ask board members to take time off for long retreats. Ensure that the retreat is productive. The best way to make it productive is by finding ways to work together to make the rest of the year more productive. The board experience doesn't have to be a burden to bear; it should be stimulating, challenging, and ultimately rewarding. Board members need to know that they're making the tough decisions for the right reasons—for all students.

Effective Staff/Cabinet Retreats

The superintendent's cabinet retreat consists of senior leadership: assistant superintendents, associates, chief communications officer, etc. This is not the school board's retreat, although you might invite the board chair to speak before the group and then take his or her leave. Be sure to include the senior communications officer; as we have noted, this person needs to be knowledgeable of everything that goes on in the district.

In any business, planning and charting directions for a specified period of time is absolutely essential and it is no different in a school district. The key to a successful retreat is the planning that goes into it. There needs to be an assessment of what has worked well previously, what has not worked as well as hoped, and what new initiatives should be undertaken. All of this needs to come together in a synergistic relationship of new ideas to get everyone on the same page. Cabinet retreats are a great time to revisit the mission, goals, objectives, and strategies—evaluating each. Typically, this retreat works best at an off-site location to allow the leadership team time to focus more broadly than they can in the day-to-day minutia-driven work agenda.

Ideally, a retreat will be scheduled to address a single goal. In any case, the fewer the goals, the better. This goal needs to capture exactly where the district needs to be. The beauty of our 95 percent goal was that all areas were key to achievement of the goal—academics, personnel, communications, facilities, social services, transportation, etc. With a single goal, each group in the district is able to concentrate on building structures in support of the single goal; the voluminous, all-encompassing document that tries to create multiple goals, objectives, and strategies for everyone will crumble under its own weight. Similarly, with a single goal, it is easier to focus and concentrate thinking at a cabinet retreat.

Selecting an off-site location for your retreat provides benefits, including an atmosphere of mutual sharing that is less threatening along with a sense of isolation and protection from daily worries and interruptions. Also, a pleasant environment away from the offices and phones can signal a new beginning. And, a neutral facilitator works best—someone with the skills and experience to keep staff from drifting, someone who can move a group through the appropriate processes and strategies.

Your facilitator should have an understanding of the educational environment so as to be comfortable with issues that require program knowledge and to be able to raise challenging questions. Homework should be given to participants in advance of the retreat, such as reading appropriate research articles and reviewing the practical work being done by practitioners. We have found that to have a rich retreat experience, such preparatory work must be done. This work also includes reviewing and analyzing previous goals and objectives, quantifying the success of each, and providing additional qualitative information that may be beneficial to refocus thinking and update personnel on the latest research and best practices.

An agenda outlining the process and activities should be provided so that all participants will have an understanding of what direction this retreat will take. Ground rules are a must, with participation by all attendees being one of the most important rules. The latter ensures ownership for the final product. If necessary, talk through impasses. Try to find common ground and never lose sight of the focus on students, teaching, and learning. In essence, all objectives and strategies to be considered should enhance students' academic performance, whether directly or indirectly.

Frequently, the press may request permission to attend staff retreats (they do attend board retreats as required by public meeting law); however, our district has typically not permitted the press to attend staff retreats. There is no public meeting law that applies and you want a setting where members feel empowered to offer their innermost thoughts on a particular topic without the threat of it being misinterpreted in the media. This means that the document produced following the retreat probably won't contain all of the ideas shared, but rather a summary of ideas later translated into recommendations. When you hold a retreat, you want the staff to speak even if what they say is politically incorrect. Allow people to be open. You're looking for honest dialogue from which you start building the goals and strategies to support your continued improvement.

We've had retreats for one day, one and a half days, two days, and some for overnight. Each retreat was driven by the items on the agenda. A heavy agenda could require overnight or two days with staff members able to go home and return the next morning. One question to address when planning how long to hold your retreat is how cohesive is your staff. A cohesive team may only need a short retreat. If you're integrating a number of new members, an overnight stay with a planned social agenda may be in order. When you're staying overnight, have dinner together so conversation can take place. After dinner, you want some planned social event—an intellectual game or a sharing exercise where everyone gets to know each other. The key is not to waste people's time; the retreat must be orchestrated and productive. A rule of thumb is never schedule retreats for more than one night. Staff will give you one night; two nights will be a difficult sell.

We have always stayed away from alcohol at retreats. We know that people may say things when alcohol flows that can be embarrassing or hurtful. At one retreat hosted by someone other than ourselves, a gentleman had more to drink than he probably should have and said some things that he believed were hidden in enough sarcasm to be humorous, but his comments created pain for the people at whom his comments were directed. He subsequently lost his job and that in turn created a rift on the staff between those who supported him and others who thought what he said had been in poor taste.

One of our best retreats was an overnight retreat, which took place forty miles out of town. Distance is important and forty miles is about right. It's close enough that people aren't driving great distances to get there or to get home. Attendees will be secure enough that they can get home in case of an emergency, yet the group is far enough away to make the venue feel different from the norm. Everything was planned with detail, and this advance planning was owned by the staff. They had provided input to the facilitator that drove the agenda and even the social events. After we arrived, time was carefully scripted. We started and stayed on time, followed the agenda, and made a pact that everyone would give their input and everyone's voice would be heard and considered.

We opened the retreat, helping all understand what our roles should be, the models we should establish for others, and why our district has a history of strong performance—leadership. We gave several examples of this leadership and it became evident that it was not a role for the timid, but for those who were willing to stretch their minds, seek excellence, and hold themselves accountable. We focused a great deal on the excellent leadership of Abraham Lincoln by way of setting the climate. We left that retreat with objectives and strategies that everyone owned and supported. If everyone couldn't own and support an objective or strategy, we didn't keep it.

Topics should not be the day-to-day issues, even in situations when a hot issue may be keeping staff busy at home. Broader issues should be considered such as student achievement, personnel recruitment and retention, safety and security, facility needs, financial concerns, and significant communication issues. The idea is to align these broad topics with strategies for achieving your goals.

Choosing the facilitator is absolutely critical. Choose a facilitator who knows a little bit about you and your system and who is somewhat familiar with the district, the state, and the standard course of study. But, choose someone who is not tied to you individually. This person needs to be tough enough and secure enough to keep everyone on track, including the superintendent.

Sometimes, an attendee will be resistant to everything and uncompromising, which can be toxic for the whole group. What is driving this person? What is the person unhappy about? If you can figure this out, you can usually get the individual back on track. It could be as simple as a prior disagreement with somebody in the group; therefore, anything the person says, this attendee will challenge just because the person put it on the table. The superintendent's job is to work with this person to see if the person can be brought back as a member of the team.

If the retreat is done well, we can build a three-year plan and then meet each year to tweak it. When done well, you will probably have a blueprint for retreats for multiple years. At subsequent retreats, we seldom needed to identify new areas for discussion; we typically followed the topics of one retreat with the next retreat. You will know if your retreat was successful when you return the second year and all you have to do is tweak.

Planning and conducting a well-managed and productive retreat requires a lot of forethought, planning, and preparation—putting your brains to work, so to speak.

WHAT YOU CAN DO TO IMPROVE

- Consider using a business leader to facilitate school board retreats and training
- Devote the necessary time—possibly two to three months of advance planning—to preparing for the retreat
- Find an off-site location and, if overnight, plan for an evening social event
- Be sure to have someone taking minutes of the meeting and recording decisions; you will need these at the next retreat

TRAINING LEADERS

Perhaps the biggest difference between a business and a school system is the amount of time and money spent on training its staff. School systems know they need to do this but there is always a shortage of money and training is sometimes overlooked. School systems may be inclined to rely on the staff to see to their own training; after all, these are all professionals and they should be vested in continuing to improve their skills. Unfortunately, relying on staff to take care of their own training needs overlooks the need there is to provide common training experiences that permit staff to develop similar understandings, processes, and ownership of roles and responsibilities in alignment with the school system's direction and initiatives.

Wake Leadership Academy

Research is very clear that successful schools and school districts can be traced to strong administrative leadership—leaders who never stop seeking answers, are never satisfied with the status quo, are creative and innovative, and who have strong interpersonal skills. After several summer seminars in a business training session, WCPSS decided to follow the business model and develop our own leaders. In 1999, we formed the Wake Leadership Academy for this purpose, a public-private partnership between Wake Education Partnership and WCPSS.

WCPSS was one of the first school districts in the state and among a few in the nation that had created its own administrative leadership program. The idea of the academy was developed based on the partnership between the school district and the Wake Educational Partnership (WEP), an advisory group of business people whose purpose is to support the mission of the school system. WEP was created approximately twenty-five years ago by the school system and has evolved into a "critical friend" of the district. WEP functions to disseminate research and best practices, challenge the status quo, improve strategic planning, expand the knowledge and skills of potential administrators, develop seminars linked to national standards, and develop a strong partnership with business.

In partnership with WEP, we decided to hire a director to run the Wake Leadership Academy. We were looking for a creative thinker—someone who wasn't anchored to anyone or any department. We wanted this person to feel free to push the envelope and thus we hired a retired superintendent with very strong instructional skills to lead this effort. The person selected convinced the committee that he was the person through exhibiting a kind of take-charge, autonomous behavior—a think-outside-the-box, go-for-the-gusto, do-your-homework kind of guy. He asked the right questions: Where do we see this program going? What's missing in our training? What should we change? How would we build this program if we had no restrictions? We decided to have this person report to the superintendent and the WEP president, which gave him the full range of working with educators and the business community.

We did not want our academy to have the standard one-size-fits-all training found in most university master's programs. This was to be a program that used achievement data to improve decision making, while also involving book study, Baldrige awareness training, facilitative leadership training, and a significant amount of follow-up training. Our initial design negotiations involved school system officials, WEP, and North Carolina State University's (NC State) Education Center. NC State, however, had their own ideas about what teachers should know, and at first they balked at our input. The university appeared to want to create a program with more theory than practicality—a program that we felt would not adequately address diversity, language issues, or classroom management. We wanted a course of study that was specifically tailored to our interests. Following this discussion, the director of the academy and WCPSS superintendent met with key people at the University of North Carolina at Chapel Hill (UNC-CH), whom we found eager to work with us. Subsequently, when NC State got wind of our talking with rival UNC-CH, NC State became more open to our ideas. As it turned out, we partnered with NC State and have been able to better ensure a pipeline of quality school leaders trained to reflect the actual needs of our school system.

The Wake Leadership Academy trains experienced teachers in the area of leadership, enlightening them about government and its role in education, and allowing them to network with other teachers, administrators, and business leaders. Administrative training is a part of the program. Once in the program, a substantial part of their coursework was paid for by the school district.

In the first cohort of approximately eighteen students, seventeen were placed in administrative positions. The "carrot" provided by the program was the master's degree, which could lead to department chair positions, grade level chairs, and assistant principal positions. Of course, with each of these positions came higher salaries. The incentives were threefold: higher education, more money, and the respect that goes along with accomplishing something significant.

From NC State's Master's in School Administration Program, associated with the Wake Leadership Academy, we developed other professional development programs to build the skill levels of our teachers. We developed programs for initially licensed teachers to ensure they had two- and three-year mentors. We also developed programs for lateral entry teachers to help them become familiar with instructional pedagogy and things for which they hadn't been trained. We created embedded professional development programs on their school campus—early mornings and late afternoons—to help the teachers when they needed help.

Businesses have been instrumental in helping finance the Wake Leadership Academy, investing $500,000 per year over a five-year period. Beginning in January 2006, the Wake Leadership Academy expanded to become the Triangle Leadership Academy to include five contingent school districts—Wake County, Durham County, Johnston County, Orange County, and Chapel-Hill-Carrboro school districts—and there is an increasing sharing of expenses among these districts. (For further details, visit the Web site for the Triangle Leadership Academy at www.triangleleadershipacademy.org/.)

Continuous Improvement Conference

To support the Wake Leadership Academy, the Continuous Improvement Conference was created. Nationally recognized consultants were brought in to present at the conference—Michael Fullen and Rick DuFour, to name a few. What started as a two-day conference grew to a five-day conference and rivaled national conferences in terms of quality sessions. The conference set the instructional tone for the year—where we were focusing our attention—and provided a great opportunity to bring administrators, teachers, and school board members together around a conference theme. All conference presenters were chosen based on their expertise in an area that supported the theme, many of whom were drawn from our own administrator and teacher leaders. Our vision for the Continuous Improvement Conference was that it would inspire and enlighten.

High Five

Obviously, the training of leaders applies to superintendents as much as anyone else, and superintendents need to look after their own interests to ensure that they stay abreast of the most current thinking and latest developments. Toward this end, the superintendents from Wake County, Orange County, Johnston County, Durham Public Schools, and Chapel Hill-Carrboro City Schools started meeting on a regular basis looking for ways to reduce the dropout rate. How do you get five school districts to work together? The answer is to find a theme that is common to all, something so challenging that it warrants the superintendents setting aside valuable time to get together with other superintendents on a regular basis. In the early stages, the superintendents met without business folks. But, it was clear to us that to make things work, we needed to work with business.

The local newspaper, *The News and Observer,* asked what we would do if we had half a million dollars. With this question, we started talking about building the capacity of our people. Then the question became: What if we could increase this funding by bringing in other business partners to make the pool $2.5 million? By April 2004, thanks to the News & Observer Publishing Company, Blue Cross and Blue Shield of North Carolina Foundation, SAS, Progress Energy, and Capitol Broadcasting Company, we had our $2.5 million and "High Five" was formed, with "High" meaning high schools and "Five" meaning five school districts. What started with five superintendents getting together to share thoughts and ideas had now morphed into another vehicle for training.

High Five focuses on improving graduation rates, reducing dropout rates, and increasing the percentage of graduates who could meet admission standards for our colleges and universities or to enter vocational fields. We had three specific goals: 100 percent graduating high school by 2013 (we recognize that this is a stretch goal); 90 percent completing college technical prep courses or college university prep courses of study by 2009 (this one is doable); and 80 percent meeting course requirements for University of North Carolina admission by 2009 (also doable). These goals drive High Five's agenda, sharing best practices in high school reform to come up with learning environments that work. The business partners were willing to put up the money because they need quality personnel to work in their businesses.

High Five has a board of directors with superintendents and business leaders who meet monthly with an executive director who was hired to develop programs. One such program was to follow the dictates of the professional learning community: train teachers to ask the right questions and then come up with instructional solutions. Out of this initiative, the five school districts have begun to focus on professional learning communities. Early college and middle college initiatives were also supported by High Five. We sought to change high schools, making them smaller, connecting them more to a theme, and tying them more directly to careers or businesses. These conversations have led to more of our high school students taking classes on the community college campuses, and in one model, for instance, graduating in five years with a diploma *and* an associate's degree.

The High Five business partners continue to provide financial and other support—publishing articles, providing free air time, running promotions on staying in school, etc. It has been a win-win partnership, with the school districts getting the support they need to promote leadership leading to greater academic achievement and improved graduation rates. Ultimately, of course, the real winners are the students. (For more information on High Five, visit www.trianglehighfive.org/.)

National Board Certified Teachers

WCPSS has the largest number of National Board Certified teachers in the entire nation, more than 1,100 in 2007–08. This is no accident. We charged our principals to encourage their teachers to go after national board certification. Between the state and the local school district, our teachers receive substantial support to pursue National Board Certification, including the cost of their registration and time away from work to prepare. We also make it a big deal for the teachers when they do receive certification, including a large reception. The biggest draw for many, of course, is a 12 percent pay increase.

In one situation, a principal was such a strong proponent in urging his teachers to pursue National Board Certification that, of his forty to fifty teachers, probably half became certified. It was a culture he created. He hired teachers who were interested in pursuing certification and who in turn encouraged others. When a school gets two or three National Board Certified teachers, pretty soon they will have five or six and it grows from there.

While many of the teachers who earn their National Board Certification remain in their roles as teachers—and this we would hope because we want to have our highest quality teachers working with our students—the National Board Certification process furthers the development of educational leaders. As your teachers improve their own skills through self-reflection, reading, and research in the effort to meet the National Board standards, these teachers also impact others in their school and the district. Many are recognized as teacher leaders among their staff and some will advance into other leadership and administrative positions.

WHAT YOU CAN DO TO IMPROVE

- Find the money in your budget to support districtwide training initiatives
- Form a leadership academy with talent from both within and outside your school system
- Hook up with the nearest institution of higher education to develop training initiatives
- Ask business leaders to support the district's initiatives to reduce school dropouts
- Challenge teachers to become nationally certified

MEASURING SUCCESS

Business leaders understand the importance—in fact, the necessity—of measuring what it is they are doing. Measurements are taken all along the production line, from monitoring the quality of the raw input and resources, to evaluating the efficiency of flow-through processes, to measuring the quality of the final output product. Measurement is also conducted with parallel processes such as marketing and public relations activities. Educators, too, are familiar with measurement. All we have to do is look at the measurements that NCLB requires. Still, there is much that we can do to improve our measurement activity, especially in regards to our processes. Are we getting the outcomes we desire for the processes and programs that we are implementing?

Evaluation and Research Focus

One of the major shortcomings in the field of education has been the use of anecdotal evidence to drive programs and policies. Many of us maintain, "It worked for me when I went to school; it'll work for today's students." Never mind that scholarship and students have changed and that many of those earlier programs failed. Businesses recognize that customers and products change constantly; because of this, they must constantly evaluate what they are doing and whom they are reaching. Educators must become like-minded—constantly evaluating our initiatives and improving these in accordance with the findings of the evaluation.

In the past, when we implemented a new program, it was frequently because someone thought it was a good idea, or it was being implemented in some other school district, or some teacher impressed us with what she was doing. We would replicate such ideas, not thinking whether it was appropriate for a particular group or school or district, simply because we never took the time to assess the needs of that population, school, or district. Many of the programs were implemented, tried, and in some cases discarded without proper evaluation of the program's purpose, goals, objectives, or outcomes—or worse—continued even when an evaluation revealed the program was without merit.

Good businesses don't rely on anecdotes to determine how to keep their business successful. Sure, they take risks and sometimes a concept fails, but they rarely move forward with a new idea without doing a considerable amount of research first. Even "New Coke," which debuted in 1985 and immediately flopped, had been subjected to evaluation.[1]

Businesses are data-driven, and one of the great lessons school systems can learn from the business community is to also be driven by data. Begin by seeking answers to the right questions. And, those answers come in the form of probing research—not anecdotes or gut feelings. Before implementing a new program, ask: Who has done it successfully in the country? Do their demographics match ours? Was there a control group? Did the research follow the appropriate methodology? Were the researchers reputable? Were they objective?

Under tight budget conditions, a school district might look to federal and state grants or foundations for new funding sources, especially for the cutting-edge, innovative initiatives that won't make the regular budget. The "need" to document *our* need in most grant proposals, along with an expectation that the proposal would implement research-proven strategies, began to teach us the importance of research and evaluation. To receive most grants, you have to conduct a needs assessment and provide data that substantiate your needs. School personnel who sought grants had to read the research and offer the grantors data-based research to show that the program they sought funding for had been proven to work under similar circumstances. And because many grants are doled out over several years, grantors usually want to see periodic evaluations proving that the money is being spent as proposed, and the program is working.

In WCPSS, the Grants Administration Office has been instrumental in helping the school district receive many millions of dollars in grant funding. When developing a grant proposal, this office creates a logic map showing the relationship among district needs, on the one hand, and services, outputs, and outcomes to be accomplished with grant funding, on the other hand. Whether in a grant proposal or simply describing how a program operates, a well-defined logic map provides guidance to program evaluation.

Whether a program is funded by a grant or locally supported, the program must be thoroughly evaluated. Is the program making a difference? Is it cost efficient? How can it be improved, or should it be sunsetted? Research personnel are needed to answer questions like these. Accordingly, school districts have started to hire people with appropriate research skills. These individuals frequently report directly to the superintendent to provide the level of autonomy they need to do their jobs (similar to the internal auditor).

With this greater emphasis on research and evaluation, many school systems began developing Evaluation and Research (E&R) departments. WCPSS started to build its E&R department in the early 1990s. Before then, we had test coordinators who were responsible for distributing and collecting test booklets and maintaining the integrity of the testing. But with the E&R department, responsibilities were expanded to include looking at test data to provide an informed opinion to the superintendent of what those data revealed about students—or, more accurately, what the data revealed about teaching and learning. Bear in mind that our test coordinators were often teachers removed from their classrooms to administer and monitor the tests. Most were outside their comfort zones when it came to program evaluation. They could tell you how many students passed or failed, but few could do more sophisticated analyses such as disaggregating data and interpreting individual student-level data. Nor could these individuals say with confidence whether any particular program was contributing more or less to changes in student achievement. Therefore, superintendents could not get complete intelligence to make an informed decision.

We knew we had to expand our E&R role. We conducted a nationwide job search to bring in a talented person who understood data and research and who could actually do research. The individual we hired and made an assistant superintendent was confident in what she knew were our needs and immediately began clamoring for a department. She wanted test coordinators, researchers with specific skills, and grant writers. If data were going to drive programs and instruction, then they needed to be properly collected, manipulated, analyzed, and interpreted for the superintendent, the board of education, the administrative cabinet, principals, and ultimately for teachers, students, and parents.

Following the hiring of this assistant superintendent, we placed the existing district test coordinator and the grants administrator under her umbrella. Subsequently, this assistant superintendent showed us that if administrators and teaching staff were to be trained to interpret and use data, then she would need to hire additional staff to do this training. Data would dictate whether we needed to buy a new instructional program, what professional development was needed for teachers, and how the budget funds should be allocated. When she arrived, no one else in the district had her skills and everyone listened when she interpreted the test data. That is, *everyone,* as she became a favorite of the administration, school board, and media. Shortly, it was actually the media that became an advocate for more data as they realized how they could use it to get smart about good programs and bad programs.

The media started to ask "Where's the research on this?" In fact, "Show me the research" became a common demand. Before implementing programs, we wanted to know who had used it and its level of success.

After we formed the Evaluation and Research department, the staff started to produce surveys and reports. For example, a question was asked, "How do parents feel about their child's school?" Before we had the E&R department, a principal might answer off the cuff, "Our students' parents are very happy." However, the board member representing that school might receive two phone calls with parent complaints and, without any real data, interpret from the calls that an uprising was afoot at the school. Was there a problem? If so, how large was it? Do our students feel safe? Do teachers feel supported? The E&R staff started constructing student, staff, and parent surveys, many of which were generated because principals wanted to know what they were doing well and where were the trouble spots. Good principals wanted to use surveys to find areas they could improve; they wanted to get ahead of their individual evaluations. Some survey questions remain the same from year to year and some change to address topical issues. Along with achievement data, survey data changed the landscape of our schools, and we can't imagine managing the school system effectively without this valuable feedback from our customers. (For more information and extensive information about how the WCPSS Evaluation and Research Department operates, including the many surveys and reports produced by the department, visit http://www.wcpss.net/evaluation-research/.)

ABC Testing

As the state developed the ABCs (Accountability, Basics, [local] Control) program (for more information on the North Carolina Department of Public Instruction ABCs program, visit http://abcs.ncpublicschools.org/abcs/), WCPSS was out front looking at its test data, disaggregating data, looking at subgroups, and figuring out what schools needed additional support. For instance, our administrators wanted to be instructional leaders who could help their teachers understand why third-grade scores were not as strong as fourth- or fifth-grade scores, and what needed to happen in third grade to change this dynamic. Our quality principals became so good at understanding data that their schools started to blossom as a result. They could pinpoint a group of students not doing well by grade level, by teacher, and sometimes by other demographic factors.

Data became a wonderful thing, but only if viewed in the correct context. For example, if schools are being ranked exclusively by percentage of students who are proficient at grade level, two schools with 90 percent proficiency rates may look identical on a data sheet. But we should ask how proficient the students were when they came to that school. For a school at 75 percent at the start of the year and 90 percent at the end of the year, is this school doing a better job than a school that started at 95 percent?

Test data that change from one year to the next should be examined closely to ensure proper interpretation. For example, test scores may plummet in a district from one year to the next. The first assumption may be that teachers aren't teaching as well. However, any number of factors may have caused a drop in scores. An influx of non-English-speaking students into the district (from 1990–2000, North Carolina's Hispanic population grew 394 percent—the largest growth of all fifty states) could have caused the scores to drop. Or, as it happened in the 2005–06 school year, the state may have renormed a test, essentially raising the bar for student performance in that subject area.

An adequately staffed E&R department can offer much to a school district. Without an E&R department, our staff would be seriously disadvantaged in their efforts to understand the state ABCs and national NCLB accountability programs. In one audit of the school district by an external group, it was noted that the WCPSS E&R department was larger than comparably-sized school districts, but it was also noted that WCPSS appeared to be making good use of the department in ways that justified its size. School leaders and boards of education would be making a mistake to undervalue the importance of evaluation and research functions, regardless of the size of the school district.

SAT When Released by the College Board

A smart E&R department helps the community understand the purpose and limitations of tests like the SAT or ACT, along with what needs to happen in the classroom to positively impact a student's score on such tests (e.g., vocabulary lessons, advanced courses, taking the pre-SAT, SAT study courses, SAT preparatory software, etc.). As WCPSS implements programs like this, year after year, almost 80 percent of WCPSS seniors take the SAT.

SAT scores used to be hit and miss in our district. One year, they dropped considerably. Through the E&R department, we brought in representatives from the Educational Testing Service (ETS), and we had them look at our testing process and offer recommendations to help us improve our students' SAT scores. Following the consultation with ETS, we conducted training with our teachers and principals; subsequently, our SAT scores have risen strikingly. In 1990, Wake County students' average SAT score was 2 points below the national average. By 2006, with 5,237 students taking the SAT (77 percent participation), our students' scores exceeded the national average by 58 points and the state average by 83 points. WCPSS was the only large urban district that consistently ranked in the top five in the state and top quartile in the nation. This has been no accident.

Benchmarking Versus Other Districts

One central question that grew out of the work of the E&R department was, how good were we? We knew what we were doing and had some idea how we were doing compared to the rest of the state, but we couldn't answer this question nationally. We had indices like the SAT, but this is not an adequate measure to compare school districts. It was the E&R department that suggested we identify a network to benchmark with other school districts demographically comparable to WCPSS. We invited these districts to meet with us and compare data and other information. The win-win for all parties was new ideas and new research—and in some cases a stroking of the ego, at least for those who came out on top. The Educational

Benchmarking Network was then formed with like school districts across the nation (e.g., Cherry Creek, CO; Brevard, FL; Duval County, FL; Cobb County, GA; Anne Arundel County, MD, etc. For more information on the Educational Benchmarking Network, visit http://www.ebndistricts.org/.).

Originally, there were seventeen benchmark districts. We would ask each other questions about suspension rates, personnel hiring practices, instructional programs, budgets, and other key issues and challenges. People in similar positions among these districts then began to share information. Through this benchmarking, we became better and started to believe we could compete with the best in the nation. This may have been the beginning of WCPSS's debut on the national stage. Other districts started trying to learn what was going on in Wake County. Unlike Coca-Cola, which understandably keeps the ingredients of its product locked in a vault, we shared our success formula with everyone. Although we've touted throughout this book how school systems should be run like good businesses, one exception is competition. While it's nice to have bragging rights to high SAT scores or other competency indicators, we have no widgets or soft drinks to offer as products that we don't want the competition to duplicate. Our "products" are competent students who can read, write, and factor polynomials. They are ready for higher education, vocations, and most importantly, to become good citizens in our community. Some competition among schools and districts is healthy, but when you have something that works and could help other students, you have a responsibility to pass it on. And the responsibility should not feel like a burden. Do it cheerfully. We would not lament if the rest of the nation raised its SAT scores by 45 points. Although we would lose our spotlight, this would further inspire us to move the bar up another notch.

In business, if companies share too much information, gaining a competitive advantage over other companies, the Federal Trade Commission would likely be investigating these companies. In public education, there is no reason why we can't share everything; we're all in the same business.

Healthy School Indicators

WCPSS has a history of trying to maintain diversity in all of its schools, whether this be diversity by academic achievement, income levels of the families, race of the student, or other factors. We believe that a healthy school district will maintain this balance among all of its schools, whether urban or suburban, newly built, or many years old. We believe there are advantages that diversity among students brings to the educational process that benefit all students regardless of race, income, family, or other characteristics. In particular, our commitment to diversity requires that we also be committed to maintaining healthy schools for all students. All schools should be equally attractive for students, parents, teachers, administrators, and the community—a source of pride in every neighborhood. And, all schools should be properly resourced. Obviously, maintaining the perfect balance at all times among all variables for all schools is not possible, but we try, and the assignment of students to schools is one of the tools used by the district.

In the past, the race of a student was one of the variables used in student assignment decisions, but race is not currently a factor. Rather, nodes in the county (akin to zip code regions, but much smaller) will be assigned to schools based on such factors as proximity to the school, the percentage of low-income families living in the node, and the percentage of students in a node performing below grade level. Compounding these factors, because of the ceaseless growth in enrollment that the district experiences every year, there is a need to assign students to new schools as they are built and opened. The assignment or reassignment of students to schools to maintain the overall health of the district is an annual challenge for both school and community.

When students are reassigned to another school, a written notice is sent to parents. Naturally, when first implemented, most parents had concerns about leaving their present school where they had become comfortable. Because we had already trained parents to be data-savvy, many started doing their homework on student assignment. They compared their children's new school with their old school. They wanted to know which school had better academic data. They used our maps to determine what percentage of students was at or above grade level. In many ways, this led some in the public to use our own data against us. As parents asked questions and, in their appeals, highlighted the negative issues of a school (lower test scores, older facility, fewer certified teachers, etc.), this led our board to look at the health of each school. Through the E&R department, we established more than one hundred indicators of a healthy school: test scores, age of facility, parental involvement, quality of teachers and staff, and diverse student body, to name just a few. With this information, we formed the Healthy Schools Review Team, led by E&R, to annually review the healthy schools indicators. When schools were found to be low on a number of healthy school indicators, then resources were adjusted, personnel scrutinized, and programs changed—all in the effort to provide every child in every school with the optimal education.

NCLB Testing

It's easy to take potshots at the federal No Child Left Behind (NCLB) legislation. It's a big target and there's a lot that is wrong with it. Take aim and you're bound to hit something. However, who will argue with the premise that we should educate all of our students to meet minimum standards of competency? Sure, you can quibble with 100 percent. Every business will accept a certain amount of failure, as none could stay in business if always trying to meet 100 percent success. The price of ensuring 100 percent success is exorbitant, and will prove to be so in education as well if this standard of the NCLB legislation is not better thought through. Left unchanged, the current NCLB standard will only lead to the day when every school and school district in the nation will be subject to take-over by the state. What would be next? Take-over by the federal government? The state and federal government's response to Hurricane Katrina should give us pause when entertaining this possibility.

When NCLB wanted to know how subgroups were doing in Wake County, we already knew the answer. We had been disaggregating data and publishing this information for a number of years and we have always supported the essential premise of No Child Left Behind. When the 2003 Goal was developed in 1998, pre-NCLB, this was developed to get all students to grade level—white, African Americans, Hispanic/Latinos, poor students, special education students, etc. Whereas NCLB adherents may believe that the legislation dictated these significant changes, we had already moved in this direction.

However, what are the chances of reaching the NCLB standard of 100 percent? There is a concern that this all-or-nothing approach puts tremendous stress on a school. We could have twenty-seven of twenty-nine groups achieving standards and still be designated as a school "in need of improvement" and the NCLB sanctions are applied. We know enough about human nature to know that you have greater success with the carrot *and* stick than with the stick alone—especially if the latter is used indiscriminately.

With NCLB, the stick approach includes sanctions, from being embarrassed in the newspaper, students being able to transfer from your campus, bringing in supplemental services, and having outsiders ultimately taking over the school. Most state departments of public instruction do not have the resources or trained personnel who can come in and effectively change a school overnight; moreover, it is possible that the school may be doing quite well by many other measures. We must be careful to not demoralize students, staff, and parents. The last scenario we want is a negative self-fulfilling prophecy—one in which we surrender, which would cause an exodus of quality staff and parents. Without a robust public education system, how will our nation fare? There will never be enough private schools, charter schools, or home schools to do the job. Imagine if public education goes down the tube, and students are distributed in all these different ways, with many not going to any school. What would happen to standards-based education then? What would happen to accountability? What would happen to 100 percent proficient? Without a robust public education system, there will be chaos.

Including NCLB and our state's ABCs program, no one has come up with the magic formula to improve student achievement, because it does not exist. Setting aside formulaic approaches, we do know school reform requires the proper personnel with the autonomy and proper resources to do their jobs—and it takes about five years to turn a school around. It's quite possible that the school will hit bottom before they turn it around. However, it has been proven that it can be done. NCLB, although it contains many commendatory attributes, wants turnaround to occur in a year or two and that's simply not possible. With the built-in guarantee that every school in the nation will ultimately fail to meet the NCLB standard for success, years from now when we look back on the NCLB legislation, we may view it as a veiled attempt to discredit public education through setting an impossible standard. We believe in stretch goals but not ones that guarantee failure. In contrast, we think 95 percent is a stretch goal and even a bit idealistic, but still something within the realm of possibility.

Most important, along with a realistic stretch goal, let's find the carrot that we can use in concert with the stick to motivate staff and student performance.

WHAT YOU CAN DO TO IMPROVE

- Ensure there is an organization function responsible for conducting program evaluations
- Form a benchmarking network with comparable school districts in the state and nation
- Identify the set of building, staff, student, and parent variables that you will annually monitor to judge the health of your schools
- Endorse the principle of NCLB that 100 percent of your students will achieve at grade level but set your own stretch goal

DOLLARS AND SENSE

It costs money to operate a business, and it costs money to operate a school district. Although the business of business is to make money and the business of schools is to educate, still, there are many similarities in how these two institutions handle money. Ultimately, the bottom line for both institutions is to get the greatest value on the dollar. Educational leaders can and must do more to help our consumers understand our budgets, and to ensure that our consumers are getting the greatest return on their investment.

Understandable Budgets

For the 1997–98 school year, the Wake County Public School System had an annual operational budget of nearly $500 million dollars. Because of enrollment growth, that budget today is over one billion dollars. Neither is a number that most people can understand, yet it is important for the public to understand the budget and how it works. But, attempts to take an understandable budget to the public can fail if not carefully prepared and presented.

Many people believe $500 million or a billion dollars should be enough to solve any problem, no matter how large and costly. But in Wake County, where 5,000–7,000 new students were entering the school system in recent years, this meant constructing new buildings, restoring old buildings, buying more buses, expanding lunch services, hiring and training new teachers, and a host of things many people in the community would never think of.

The first reaction of school critics to any request for additional school funding often is to complain about wasted money in the "bloated bureaucracy" of education. This continues to be the case even in Wake County with its exceptional growth. After all, the school system is part of the government and most adults remember news accounts such as learning the government has spent $600 on a toilet seat. The phrase "bloated bureaucracy" gets traction in the media looking to stir up a controversy and in the community for those looking to throw stones. It only increases the pressure on school leaders if school financial information is hard to access or understand. Thus, it becomes a must for school systems to not only make the budget information readily available, but also easily understandable.

In late 1999, after Wake County's first bond defeat in history, CPA Tom Oxholm came aboard to look over our annual budget. The annual budget that we presented to the school board each March for the following fiscal year was always thorough and accurate, and met federal, state, and county requirements for information. The budget and accounting staff were very dedicated and worked hard to compile it. But, the budget document itself was over 1,000 pages and weighed almost as much as a newborn baby. It contained comprehensive details on how each dollar would be spent, but it had neither a table of contents nor an index to guide anyone through it. It did have a heart-warming introduction by the superintendent that focused on the history of the school system, its accomplishments, and a statistical section that compared our county and school system spending with other counties in the state. However, it contained very little narrative about why certain expenditures were imperative, no summary of changes from the past, no frequently asked questions, and no section on savings or improvements initiated by the system. Basically, it was a navigational nightmare, and even the school board had trouble understanding where to find the information they needed to make decisions. Because it was so large and unwieldy, only 200 copies of it were printed to save money.

Tom helped the district redesign the document to make it user friendly. He eliminated much of the fluff and made it easy for anyone interested to find information they might want to know. The introduction now includes a summary of what is found in the rest of the document, along with the important changes in the school system's request for funding. The financial section clearly details discontinued programs and the savings from them. It also shows the increases needed, due to the growth in the number of students and school buildings added to house them. New programs are explained in detail and a business case is made for why they are needed. The statistical section includes comparisons with school systems not only in our state but others in the south that are recognized for excellence. And, the whole budget document is available on the school system Web site for anyone to peruse, including a section for frequently asked questions (www.wcpss.net/budget).

The size of the budget document has been significantly reduced in pages and weight, and it still complies with all federal and state regulations. Fewer copies are actually printed (saving money), but everyone has access to it because it is posted online. It is now easier to navigate and understand. The county commissioners, as well as the public, have a much better understanding of what has happened since the last budget, including where cuts have been made and when and why new money is being requested.

Critics still complain from time to time about a bloated bureaucracy, but now they complain mainly about the big school system needs, such as bond issues for buildings. The system now can reply proactively with already published information on savings and cuts, presented so that any interested user can find what they want, all of which contributes to a higher level of trust for the school system.

The Budget Request Process

In the spring of 2000, Tom reviewed the budget as a first-time board member. He had spent years studying budgets for information, but this was his first look at a budget as the source of next year's funding.

Because in North Carolina the school board does not have taxing authority, it is the board members' job to ask the county commissioners for what we thought teachers and students needed. However, the county commissioners had been very critical of the school board members for what they believed was a lack of accountability to the public. Of course, this is how our state's constitution wants it done—the school board asks for what it believes is needed and the county commissioners fund what they think is necessary. How well this works depends on your point of view and the county you live in. Compared to the nation, North Carolina ranks low in per-pupil spending for K–12 education and the state also ranks low in academic performance. Maybe the old adage is true; you get what you pay for.

This time, with Tom's leadership over three marathon budget sessions, the school board reviewed in detail the budget document, first for cuts in spending on a line-by-line basis, and then the varied revenue sources. When we finished, we had "saved" $5.5 million and had reduced what the county commissioners would need to request in a property tax increase request from three cents to two cents per hundred dollars of valuation. That was the good news. The bad news was that we had not thought to communicate our working process to the commissioners. They still didn't trust us and no tax increase was supported.

That experience opened our eyes to a communication gap that we had with the commissioners. School district leaders discussed this concern, and Tom suggested that before we ask for an increase in taxes, we should show the commissioners that we really cared about accountability through engaging the commissioners in the process. Tom also brought to our attention that alternative sources other than the government can provide revenue, and we began to pursue them.

Alternative Revenue Sources

The single largest revenue source we ever added was an exclusive distribution contract with Pepsi. Over the term of a five-year contract, Pepsi added about $3 million to total school revenues. About half of that was captured by the school system, but new monies were passed through to every school as well. Before this contract, each school arranged their own provider contract and the school board annually approved each one individually. The schools were bound by certain rules of operation and access for children. Essentially, all we wanted to do was to combine the contracts and offer them to the highest bidder, probably Pepsi or Coca-Cola. We were about the thirtieth school system in the country to do this and one of the largest. From our staff research, the winning bid we received from Pepsi was better than the contracts in place at other school districts. Then Associate Superintendent Del Burns made sure that every school received at least what they had received prior to the new contract. Beverage vending machines were already in place throughout the schools; the only thing new about this contract was that we would use only Pepsi products, because Pepsi offered the highest bid. Sure, our critics could complain that we were touting Pepsi products, but this argument was minor when compared with the funds we received to support the instructional program.

Although little would change as far as available beverages for the students, from the public's reaction, you might have thought we were not interested in the health of our students. Childhood obesity is a genuine concern throughout the nation, and our contract shed light on the fact that children had access to soft drinks at school. In fact, not one additional vending machine was going to be added to a school campus, nor any hours of operation changed (the vending machines are only on during certain hours before and after school); yet, this contract pointed out that the schools were making money by selling children soft drinks that could be damaging to their health. It was a close board vote, but all during the process, no one moved to remove the machines from the campuses. Nor have there been any motions for their removal during the renewal process five years later.

In light of growing concerns about the dietary habits of our nation's children and youth, whether the district will continue this particular contract remains to be seen. Our point is that a school district should always be open to the possibilities inherent in exclusive contracts.

In later budget years, money was again tight. After we had successfully lobbied the board for the ability to add citizens to board committees, in 2002 the board asked our finance committee to look into other sources of revenue and make recommendations to the board about avenues that might be worth pursuing. Over several months, we investigated many sources and ended up recommending to the board of education the following possible revenue enhancing alternatives:

- Obtain systemwide exclusive athletic clothing and equipment contracts
- Provide major retailer (Wal-Mart, Lowe's, grocery stores) rebate programs
- Sell naming rights to school facilities
- Sell advertising space on school property/buses and in school system publications
- Offer leases of school property for cell phone towers
- Consolidate purchasing of school supplies, office equipment, vending machines, etc.
- Make available school system programs, professional development, and expertise to smaller school systems for a fee
- Hire a full-time development officer to lead these initiatives and other programs such as annual fund raising, grant solicitation, endowment recruitment, etc.

To date, none of the recommendations have been acted upon, but this is not to say that school districts should give up on seeking alternative funding sources. Whether one or another option is actually developed may be a matter of timing, who's on the board of education, or how dire the financial situation is, among other scenarios.

Saving Money by Acting Like a Business

A public school system is no more a business than any other governmental entity. But that does not mean that some things cannot be done to imitate the way businesses operate. After all, who would complain about an efficient bureaucracy?

A school system is a bureaucracy with a goal to educate children to be well-prepared citizens for society. Every school system's mission statement will include some aspect of that concept and school systems attract trained educators to accomplish that mission. Typically, some of those educators progress from teaching or counselor positions to school-based administrators and finally to system administrators. In doing so, their experience adds to their abilities to run schools effectively. However, where along the line do school administrators gain the experience to be accountants and budget managers?

Making a profit, cutting costs, and saving money are concepts that are not taught in college to education majors, nor do individuals usually develop these skills voluntarily. And why should they? There is little incentive in government-funded entities to save money. So, who can make the decision to do things differently to save money? As a CPA, Tom was able to identify a number of things that WCPSS was not doing that offered substantial opportunities to save money. The only challenge was that he had to convince the person in charge of each particular area to try something new.

Insurance

WCPSS has more than 16,000 employees. Prior to re-examination, insurance benefits provided to them included workers compensation, medical insurance, and dental insurance. Almost every business of more than a few hundred employees investigates self-insurance as a cost-saving measure.

Insurance is by its nature about 40 percent administration costs, and self-insurance saves money in a few ways. First, it reduces the administration costs charged by the insurance company by hiring a third party administrator who specializes in low cost administration. Second, it hopefully reduces the overall pool of risks by working to keep participants healthy (managing your own risk instead of participating with others). And third, the self-insurer retains the use of its money while claims are being administered.

In WCPSS, the health plan is self-insured by the state government so changes to that system were not available. But the workers compensation plan and dental plan were commercially insured. Starting first with the dental plan, WCPSS converted to self-insurance, saving about 25 percent of the then $3 million annual cost. Then, the school system converted its workers compensation plan to self-insured, saving more than $1 million per year. Those savings were kept by the system and did not revert to the state or local government. The funds were used for academic programs to help students. Other school systems in North Carolina have started saving money in this way as well. If the state were even more aggressive, it could self-insure these areas as well as the health plan, saving money for everyone.

Payroll

Teachers are typically teaching in school for ten months of the year. They may be paid their salary entirely during those ten months, or they may elect to spread it over twelve months. Many do the latter, which creates payroll processing nightmares. Some teachers leave and never return; they change banks; they change their minds; they change careers. Figuring out where the money was to go was often a bureaucratic headache. Although, by deferring ten months of pay over twelve months the school system was able to retain more money longer, the savings were offset by the many errors that occurred in the system. Not only were some teacher accounts difficult to reconcile, but also fiscal errors (such as paying teachers one-tenth instead of one-twelfth of their pay) occurred. These errors would be detected by state payroll audits after they were paid, but they were often irretrievable, causing a loss to the system.

Payroll was a huge problem with a simple solution. The answer was the business way of doing things—outsource it so that everyone is better off. Dr. Del Burns and his staff in the payroll/accounting department worked with the State Employees Credit Union to take all the funding for those electing the twelve-month option to set up an account for them. The Credit Union handled the payment scheduling at their own risk and enrolled thousands of new customers. The employees received what they requested and also kept the interest income on delayed funds. And, the school system got rid of a big money-losing headache while also reducing personnel needs—a win-win for all. WCPSS was the first in the state to try it and many have now duplicated it—saving lots of taxpayer money statewide.

The above examples were easy for a CPA or financially trained corporate person to spot and the associate superintendent for administrative services, Del Burns, was willing to think outside the box. This is why we believe it's so important to bring in experts for specialty skill sets. Put business people in charge of the "business," and have a CPA help you with your budget. Yes, it means bringing in outsiders, but these outsiders can help the school system not only do its business more effectively and efficiently, but also save money that could be used for educating students. Perhaps the biggest challenge is to find a qualified candidate willing to take on a bureaucracy type job for the amount of money a school system can afford to pay. One of the first accomplishments under the current superintendent Del Burns's leadership was to find and hire this type of person to be the district's chief business officer.

School Bonds

Wake County has had such steady growth in population that it has been necessary to issue debt every three to four years to construct schools. The county is conservatively run like many in North Carolina and it has preserved its rare AAA bond rating all during this time. The county commissioners are charged with the task of raising the money, and they like to do it without raising the ire of the voters by associating new taxes to pay for the new debt. And therein lies the never-ending battle.

In the last twenty-five years, the school system has more than doubled in student enrollment. Sales taxes and property taxes—the county's only two reliable sources of revenue—have been growing steadily as well. Since the state legislature controls the sales tax rate, the county looks to the property taxes for its revenue to cover everything, including debt payments. Between the school board and the county commissioners, the question always comes down to this: How large can the new school bond be without raising taxes?

Let's review some facts. Wake County is the second wealthiest county in North Carolina. It is the highest ranked location in the country for percentage of college-educated citizens. It has the lowest property tax rate of any urban county in North Carolina by 10 percent. And, it is widely regarded as one of the best large public school systems in the country. So, why would it be hard to pass a school bond associated with a tax increase? Some possible reasons include the following:

- Generally speaking, no one likes to see taxes increase.
- Those who will support a bond may be more passive about voting than those who oppose the bond.
- Much of the public may be misinformed about public education, even the public with children in our schools.
- A majority of the public does not have children in the public school system (about 70 percent).

- Some of the public with school-age children will be critics of the school system.
- A percentage of the public will always perceive any government agency (including schools) as an inefficient bureaucracy.

Every single bond vote in the last twenty-five years has faced these same factors and all passed but one. The one that failed asked for an 8-cent tax increase and was voted down in 1999. In 2006, a $970 million bond passed with a 4.7-cent tax increase with 53 percent of the vote—the largest successful school bond approved in the nation at that point in time.

Based on this experience, we generally know what makes for a successful school bond. First, no tax increase. The problem with this approach for Wake County and other high-growth areas is that the school system gets further and further behind with each successful bond. For it to have no tax increase, the bond is cut to such a size that by the time the new buildings are constructed and the old ones renovated, the new growth has outpaced the improvements. Even the $970 million 2006 bond was only half of what was actually needed.

An organized support system dedicated to passing the school bond is important. In Wake County, this has always been a group called Friends of Wake County, organized solely for the purpose of passing school bonds. It is led by business leaders in the community who raise the money necessary to promote the bonds through advertising and disseminating the information and statistics that make the case for our need.

The opposition to a bond is significant even in times when no tax increase is required, although no-tax-increase bonds have often passed with a 75–80 percent approval rate. However, when a tax increase is required, the opposition truly comes out in force. Every anti-tax or anti-public school group unifies and does its best to create as much confusion as possible. Often, these groups insist that there is a "better way," though they fail to produce a viable alternative. Our critics would disagree and say they have viable solutions, but these solutions invariably create different problems that will be even more costly in time. Regardless, our critics heap criticism on the school system for any number of problems, real and imagined. Basically, they try to cause an uninformed voter to think that maybe it would be safer to vote "No" so as to send the school leaders a message. It worked in 1999. It did not work in 2006.

Leaders in the school system cannot actively campaign or raise money to promote the bond referendum. Still, we recognize that a bond vote is just like any other political vote in the country—the winner is able to persuade the unbiased voter by getting out a simple and memorable message. In 1999, that was done by the opponents claiming there was a "Better Way."

The school district's leaders saying it was "for the children" did not resonate with voters in 1999. In 2006, what worked was telling the voters that the schools had to be built and that bonds were the cheapest way to pay for it. Of course, getting out that message cost approximately $500,000 of privately contributed funds. Thank you, Friends of Wake County.

The media present a unique problem in any bond campaign and can be the biggest roadblock in the contest for passing school bonds. Their mission on paper may be to present both sides of an issue fairly, but their objective is to stimulate public interest. They can do this by highlighting the controversial aspects of an issue, thus fueling the conversation and debate. Even one negative headline can be very detrimental to the school district's interests. Many people will read the headline and may not read the full story. On the whole, Wake County's local media are very supportive of the public school system, especially editorially. When a bond is being voted on, school leaders will need the support of many advocates in and out of the schools, especially business people, to continually counter the adverse effects of any negative headline.

School bonds are usually the best way to pay for the future use of school buildings—just like a mortgage on a home. Passing them is always going to be a challenge if a tax increase is sought. The message must be simple, clear, and resonate with the public.

School Construction

After twenty-five years spent following school construction trends in a rapidly growing location, our school leaders are quite practiced and competent in this area. Of course, when it comes to any phase of education, many people believe they too are experts.

Back in the 1980s, when the need first arose for a significant number of new schools to keep up with the growth, the county commissioners decided that the school system did not have the expertise to manage that much construction and the related projects. They essentially insisted that the system hire a consulting firm to run the school construction process. Subsequently, the district contracted with Heery International.

Ten years later, the county commissioners (a different group) thought that too much money was being wasted on external consultants and we should be able to manage the construction projects internally. We then hired a number of talented Heery personnel and implemented an internally managed construction program. Now, another ten years have passed and questions about the school district's ability to manage a construction program of nearly $1 billion have resurfaced. Another change, perhaps to outside management, may be on the horizon. History may repeat itself.

The 2000 school construction package was about $500 million. The construction period coincided with a soft construction market. Bids on school projects were numerous and cheap. Millions of dollars were saved because of this competition. By the end of the four years, nearly $50 million was available for additional projects. The conclusion of some commissioners was that the bond information had been inflated to make it easy to save money. Their answer was to use as construction estimates the finished costs for the 2000 bond project to determine estimates for the 2003 bond requirements. But, when this next bond was presented, the recession was over. It coincided with a $3.1 billion dollar university construction bond and construction bids were high. The school district bond, now being completed, was unable to do all that it was forecast to do. And a major part of the reason was the county commissioners funding for it included $50 million in savings on the projected construction costs. Their reasoning was obvious—you cannot trust the school system to provide good estimates. So, a number of projects were deferred and not done. You can imagine how well that played out in the public for the latest 2006 bond issue. We heard cries of incompetence, calls for outside management, and demands to cut the inefficient bureaucracy.

After all these years and the back-and-forth discussions, we are beginning to think that one group should raise the money to build our schools and be in charge of spending it. That way, the accountability lies with one party, eliminating the ability of the other side to point fingers. So, what will it be? A school board with taxing authority or county commissioners building schools? Because the state legislature controls taxing authority, and they seem to like the current system, we don't see much likelihood of an imminent change. That's too bad, because it might well be the smart decision—it is what almost every other school system in the nation does. So, then, maybe we should let the county commissioners build the schools. Would this be heresy or lunacy—opinions that many of our colleague educators hold? Maybe not, and here is why.

Everyone wants a new school that works well and looks nice, but not too fancy. So, if the commissioners started building schools that were cheaper and *looked* cheaper, they would hear from teachers, parents, and neighbors. And nobody screams louder than parents who think their child is getting short-changed. Many in the community will not like building cheaper schools, including the elimination of ball fields, art classrooms, auditoriums, etc. The commissioners are not used to vocal citizens in the numbers that the school board deals with regularly. Let them build one substandard school, and they would not make that mistake again. Correcting an error in construction is always more expensive than getting it right the first time.

If the commissioners wanted to build more high-rise schools on less land, eliminate ball fields, auditoriums, and art rooms—all in the name of saving money—let them shoulder the responsibility. The outcry would probably be overwhelming. But if it is not, then a new community standard would be set. If the commissioners wanted to delay costly but badly needed renovations on old school buildings, again, the community that sends children to those buildings would let them know their concerns. Delay or reduce technology? You get the idea. And, certainly, in this type of arrangement there would need to be safeguards to assure compatibility with the educational programs the board of education mandates. Nonetheless, if the accountability lies with one elected body, the result will be what the community wants.

Some school administrators and boards of education may think this is a bad idea. They believe that once control is given up, it can never be recovered. A sunset provision in the agreement can take care of that. But perhaps you just have to trust that if accountability works in other communities, it will possibly work here too.

With the county commissioners building schools, the fact is that some things could definitely work better even if nothing is done differently in terms of school locations or design. First, the county would not have to pay sales tax on its purchases while the school system does. That saves 3 percent of construction materials right there, enough to build an entire new school in our district. Second, all the developers have to work with the county on lots of projects. When the county is unhappy with performance, the developer is going to respond rapidly for fear of losing a good relationship with the county (and its inspectors). They cannot do that and have their business survive. Third, the community would believe that the construction management was being done better, because the county is perceived as being better at business than are educators.

After the school board gets used to the idea of someone else managing construction, their own job will be so much easier they may never want the construction management back. They could actually focus on educational issues instead of facilities. People who would never run for the school board because of the time commitment would now be able to consider it—including more business people. It is another one of those win-win opportunities that is clear to a business person but cloudy and filled with doubt for an educator. It probably won't happen, but it would be interesting to see. In truth, we believe WCPSS has been a very good steward of the county's money and maintaining our schools, but there's no question that it's a challenging task. Maybe we should let the commissioners have their turn. As this book goes through its final editing, the business community is demanding this very issue be examined closely by the Board of Commissioners and

Education. The growth in the community is not subsiding, the conflicts over construction continue, and the need for more operational dollars is getting drastic. Perhaps they will decide to give it a try!

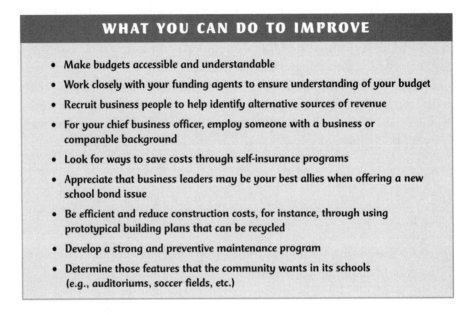

WHAT YOU CAN DO TO IMPROVE

- Make budgets accessible and understandable
- Work closely with your funding agents to ensure understanding of your budget
- Recruit business people to help identify alternative sources of revenue
- For your chief business officer, employ someone with a business or comparable background
- Look for ways to save costs through self-insurance programs
- Appreciate that business leaders may be your best allies when offering a new school bond issue
- Be efficient and reduce construction costs, for instance, through using prototypical building plans that can be recycled
- Develop a strong and preventive maintenance program
- Determine those features that the community wants in its schools (e.g., auditoriums, soccer fields, etc.)

NOTE

1. Malcolm Gladwell in his book, *Blink: The Power of Thinking Without Thinking* (Little, Brown and Company, 2005), provides an interesting account of how the Coca-Cola Company was led astray by market research that was too narrowly constrained, being based largely on a sip test. One implication for education leaders is that there are many forms of evaluation and it behooves us to "triangulate" our data—to look at a situation or program from multiple perspectives so as to gain the most complete picture possible.

Leadership and Heart

And remember, my sentimental friend, that a heart is not judged by how much you love, but by how much you are loved by others.

—The Wizard in *The Wizard of Oz*

When we think of heart, we think of our emotions, values, and morals as distinguished from the intellectual nature. For instance, someone said to have a "heart" might be a person with a generous disposition.

In the story of Oz, it is the Tin Woodman who wished to have a heart, and in the business of education we want employees, students, parents, and community to have and demonstrate heart. To be successful in education, business, or life, one needs an ability to connect with people, which is frequently demonstrated through interpersonal skills. Strong interpersonal skills separate the master teacher from the average teacher and manifest themselves in observable behaviors such as where the teacher physically stands in the classroom; the wait time the teacher provides for students to answer a question; positive reinforcement the teacher provides for students; elimination of put downs; a demand that students respect each other; a sense of humor; and empathy with high expectations for each student.

For example, research indicates that teachers who wait more than seven seconds for student responses are evidencing a belief that the students know the answer; waiting less than that time is seen as a belief the students don't know the answer. Now ask yourself, how important is it that teachers provide clues that they believe a student knows an answer? Doing so, is this heart? We think so.

Without question, students can sense if a teacher believes in them. The students know this and, furthermore, have concerns about whether their teacher even likes them. How well a student will perform academically in the classroom and follow instructions such as turning in homework can be frequently traced back to how the student views his personal standing in the eyes of the teacher. How many times have we heard "my teacher doesn't like me" as a reason a student does poorly in a class? And, how many times do we dismiss this as an explanation for a student's failure? But, maybe we need to take the student's expression at face value—take it to heart, so to speak. The teacher who models heart by caring and respecting others is able to take advantage of teachable moments to foster the kind of citizenship that has made this country the envy of the world. Modeling heart as adults, we can teach brotherhood and the value of service, helping young people know we all are our brothers' keeper.

We can give many other examples of heart—the sharing of a table in the cafeteria at lunch; helping a student up who trips and falls; friendly banter with different ethnic groups; not participating in racial stereotyping or hateful language; and leveling the playing field for the impoverished student. Think how different our world would be if everyone modeled heart. Would liberals and conservatives better respect their differences of opinion? Would religions be more tolerant of different beliefs and practices? Would government officials be more responsive to the public? Would we still be combating racism, sexism, and classism in twenty-first-century America? The heart we display in how we treat our teachers, how teachers treat students and parents, and how the public treats educators has everything to do with our survival and prosperity as a nation.

Being in education, you would think that we have cornered the market on heart—but sometimes we may stray as leaders. For instance, pressures to meet state and national accountability standards may cloud our thinking, contribute to distress, and make it hard for our heart to shine through. But even in business, the quality leader understands the importance of heart. Business people want happy, productive employees (teachers) creating the highest quality product (students) and developing satisfied customers (parents). While business leaders may focus on the employee, educational leaders will need to keep teachers and parents in their hearts as well as students. Students, teachers, and parents all matter the most.

STUDENTS MATTER MOST

Students matter the most because they are the products of the education business. Without excellent products, the school will go out of business. In business, customers find another supplier; in education, families seek other alternatives such as home school, charter school, or private school. In manufacturing, raw materials are purchased and nothing is wasted. In education, the child entering kindergarten is a "raw material" and thirteen years later we do not want to have wasted any of that child's potential. Business and educator leaders have the same task—making their products the best they can be, each and every one of them.

Economics, Not Race, Is the Decisive Factor

Although few educators today will argue that a student's ability to learn is a function of that student's race, many maintain that minority students, especially the Native American, African American, and Hispanic/Latino student, are at risk for school failure in the American system of public education. Certainly, racial issues have created many challenges for educators in the history of American education and it is true that it takes considerable good will for people of different races to come together and work for a common good. And yet, a student's economic level may be an even more powerful predictor of success in our educational systems than race.

Low-income students do not have many of the same advantages as students with higher incomes such as convenient access to the latest computer technology in the home, exposure to travel and a variety of educational experiences outside of school, and/or numerous books and magazines in the home. Typically, for low-income families, the educational level of the parents is, on the whole, less than that for the rest of the adult community. In our district, when we disaggregate data, we have found that the students' income level is more strongly correlated with achievement than race of the student.

Sharing the Challenge—Economic Integration Policy

Prior to 1976, Wake County had two school systems: Raleigh City and Wake County. By 1976, the idea of merger, though unpopular, was being entertained because the city system was losing white middle-class students to the county, and the county system was bulging at the seams with increasing enrollment. There were numerous over-enrolled schools in the county and a need for more capacity, along with under-enrolled schools in the city with some schools closed or recommended for closure. Desegregation of our city and county schools was a primary impetus for merger, as there was the recognition that court involvement was a potential reality if local action was not taken to ensure that the schools were acceptable under the law.

How the Raleigh City and Wake County school systems came to merge into a single countywide school district is a story of its own. Suffice it to say that accomplishing the merger required foresight, courage, heart, brains, and the commitment of some very dedicated people to an idea that everyone deserved a quality school.

We knew that the merger would not by itself ensure that schools would be racially balanced, primarily due to housing patterns. Following the merger, leadership in the school district then implemented a 15/45 policy that was designed to have no less than 15 percent minority students enrolled in a school and no greater than 45 percent minority enrolled in a school. The idea was to mirror the district's minority student population, which was about 30 percent. Because of entrenched, long-standing housing patterns, the 15/45 standard required substantial bussing of students (primarily minority) to suburban schools and some transportation of majority students to inner city schools. Student assignment became a factor for school leaders to decide: What students would be assigned to what schools?

Following the merger, the WCPSS assignment plan helped to accomplish desegregation by redrawing school boundaries and factoring in variables such as the racial composition of the neighborhood, the proximity of schools to each other, and bus transportation patterns. Even with transportation and the reassignment of students by the district, some schools in the inner city were still not able to meet the threshold of the 15/45 policy. While the district's assignment plan adopted by the board was strong enough and equitable enough to satisfy federal civil rights officials, we were not satisfied. For all students—regardless of where they lived, their economic circumstances, or their color of skin—to have an equitable chance for the highest quality education, we needed to do better at diversifying our schools. No school in our district should be full of the poor, comprised of only a single race, or forgotten in the competition for resources.

To remedy the white student deficit in inner city schools, the district's leadership researched and chose to implement a network of magnet schools in the district, creating the first five magnet schools during the years 1976–1982. Beginning with the 1982–1983 school year, WCPSS dramatically expanded its magnet schools and implemented its Schools of Choice plan, establishing twenty-eight magnet schools throughout the district. Each magnet school would have a base attendance zone and would make a number of seats available to lure other students from designated attendance zones especially where white students were the majority. Magnet schools typically were theme-focused (e.g., Gifted and Talented, Arts and Science, Technology, Classical Studies, etc.) with an array of elective courses for students to choose and students outside the schools' base attendance nodes could apply to attend.

The 15/45 standard has never been an absolute policy; the district makes exceptions for students based on extenuating circumstances or hardships. When there were more applicants than seats available at a magnet school and the overall applicant pool was not sufficiently diverse, the district employed a weighted lottery with the race of the student being a factor in the lottery until the year 2000. On the whole, the magnet plan has been very successful resulting in a strong core of inner city magnet schools. The magnet program has also created opportunities for the district to try out innovative instructional programs and introduced a healthy competition among our schools. Still, there have always been concerns about the number of magnet seats available, who got in and who didn't, whether the magnet schools were skimming bright students from other schools, the disproportionate bussing of African American students, and a perception that resources were being taken away from the regular schools to support the magnet schools.

A task force was created to review the health of all the district's schools and functioned under a title of the Healthy Schools Task Force. The task force viewed each school in the district as a part of a much larger system and compared each school to the community of all schools. Previously, we have mentioned how this task force identified over one hundred variables that were thought to be associated with healthy school functions. From this collection, a summary recommendation of the task force was that all schools should be held to the same standards:

- A diverse student body
- Strong and effective leadership
- Highly trained and effective staff
- High academic achievement for all students
- Strong parental support and commitment
- Strong community support and commitment

- Attractive and appropriate learning facility
- A safe, orderly, and inviting learning environment

In the 1990s, race became less of a factor in making student assignment decisions to magnet and traditional schools. The 1990s were marked by the increasing departure of the courts as the driver of school desegregation. As challenges to race as a major consideration for school assignment mounted, the courts seemed more reluctant to push this issue. By 1998, race of the student in the district was being considered only in the narrowly tailored fashion as recommended by the federal Office of Civil Rights. Following the courts dismantling of the Charlotte-Mecklenburg School System's bussing program, the Wake County Board of Education met on January 10, 2000, and directed the district administration to develop student assignment factors and priorities needed to maintain a diverse student population, but ruled out racial balance as a basis for reassignment. This led to the assignment of attendance nodes to a particular school based on the nodes' socioeconomic composition (as measured by percentages of students in that node receiving free and reduced-price lunch) and the academic achievement of students in a node (as measured by the percentage of students in a node performing below grade level on North Carolina's End-of-Grade tests in Grades 3–8). These new indices of diversity in student enrollment—income and achievement—are that the percentage of free and reduced-price lunch students at any school should be no greater than 40 percent and the percentage of students performing below grade level at any school to be no greater than 25 percent.

There is a strong commitment among school district leaders—board members, administrators, principals, and teachers—to the idea that all students matter. Every student should have his or her chance to succeed, all students should have highly qualified teachers, and all students should have appropriate resources and equitable facilities. District leaders appreciate that the diversity of the student body is an essential ingredient to seeing this commitment through.

Character Education Program

There is no argument among educators or business people that character counts. When business people speak with educators, we're told over and over again that the character of the employee is extremely important and we're implored to instill good character traits in our students. Whether referred to as character traits or life skills or something else, school leaders will often seek to implement character education programs along with the standard curriculum of reading, writing, and mathematics. When initiating such an undertaking, a question that will invariably arise is, "What are the character traits that we want to teach and reinforce?" One person's list of traits reflecting good character will differ from the next person; moreover, these lists will likely change over time from generation to generation. If a character education program is to take hold and thrive in a school district, it is important that there is a consensus of opinion regarding what traits will be emphasized. For us in Wake County, we knew that that consensus would be found in the community's values.

In the 1990s, leaders in the school district recognized a need to reinforce improved behavior among students and standardize expectations of student behavior across the district. Business leaders were also emphasizing the importance of character. Following the leadership of one member of our board of education, in December 1993, a task force was assembled made up of representatives among parents, staff, students, business people, the faith community, and others. This task force was charged with the responsibility of identifying a set of character traits that were representative of our community and that would allow us to design a character education program that would complement and reinforce the standard course of study.

There were thirty-two members who made up the task force and all were encouraged to name character traits that were important to academic as well as personal success. As previously noted in Chapter 2, the initial round of discussion resulted in the identification of sixty-four traits. In subsequent discussions, this list was combined and winnowed to thirty-two, then sixteen, and finally eight. All thirty-two members of the task force endorsed this final set of eight character traits: courage, good judgment, integrity, kindness, perseverance, respect, responsibility, and self-discipline. The process of thirty-two diverse individuals—representing gender, religion, income, ethnicity, and race—unanimously endorsing a set of character traits sent a powerful signal to the community and schools that these eight traits were fundamental to the business of education and reflected the values of our community.

Subsequently, an individual was hired by the school district to develop ways and means to integrate character education in all subject areas. The outcome was a program designed to model behavior and take advantage of teachable moments. The program was not designed to be an add-on to the curriculum—one more thing that teachers would have to fit into an already full curriculum—but was instead designed to be integrated across the curriculum. The main focus areas were English/language arts, social studies, healthful living, guidance, and vocational and technical education. Sample lesson plans demonstrating how the eight character traits could be integrated within the state's standard course of study were provided. And, the program was designed to also take advantage of those other times and locations during the school day when character could be featured, including student recognition programs, bulletin boards, and newsletters.

Training in character education principles and practices with teachers and administrators was conducted by the school district's staff development office with the expectation that modeling the eight character traits would be the norm in all schools. Furthermore, character education was made a part of each principal's evaluation—how well principals integrate character education in their school's program of instruction and cocurricular activities is rated, providing for a measure of accountability with respect to implementing the program.

The character education program has matured over the years to include a mission statement, definitions of each character trait, and examples of program objectives. In April 2005, the board of education put into policy what had been practiced in the schools for the previous twelve years, giving final approval to Character Education Policy 5130. This policy reflects the eight character traits adopted by the school district in 1993 and focuses on curriculum, school climate, and community involvement as core components of the program.

In the years since 1993, WCPSS has received numerous accolades and recognitions for its character education program, including the entire district being recognized by the National Character Education Center as a National School District of Character in 1999. In 2003, one of the district's elementary schools was recognized as a National School of Character and a teacher in Wake County was named the National Character Education Middle School Teacher of the Year.

Perhaps one of the most impressive recognitions came in 2001 when North Carolina Governor Mike Easley signed into law House Bill 195, the "Student Citizenship Act of 2001," which requires schools to implement character education programs: *Each local board of education shall develop and implement character education instruction with input from the local community. The instruction shall be incorporated into the standard curriculum and should address the following traits. . . .* In House Bill 195, the state names the same eight traits that WCPSS first identified in 1993. It is said that imitation is the most sincere form of flattery.

After thirteen years, the district's character education program continues to thrive. The original eight traits have stood the test of time and they are now incorporated in both the student and staff handbooks. We don't mean to imply that we have identified the single best set of traits to implement in a character education program. Rather, what we want to emphasize is the process by which we identified these eight traits—the whole community was involved. It is this process of involving the whole community that shows heart. While it is difficult to attribute cause and effect to any single program, we are confident that we are realizing improved school climate, better student discipline, and more positive staff attitudes.

Although the program was originally designed for students, there is no question that it also has an impact on school staff. If educators expect students to demonstrate good character traits, the educators themselves must model these same traits, and what teachers model speaks volumes about their character. Teachers' hearts are not expressed primarily in what they say, they are expressed in what they do—the comforting hand on the shoulder, the inquiry when the student looks sad, the concern when they know there's trouble in a student's life, the willingness to stay after school to help the struggling student, the after-hours phone call to parents to share news about a student, and even the trinkets and supplies they purchase with their own money.

Student Council Presidents and the Superintendent

The successful CEO will tell you that the key to his or her success is a willingness to listen to stakeholders. If they listen well, information will be shared that is valuable when making key decisions about the operation and financial aspects of the company. Frequently, they will hear some information that will not make them happy, but hearing the truth is the first step to resolving any issue. In the business of education, we maintain that the student is one of the key stakeholders. This should be self-evident—who else has more to gain?

Stakeholders provide intelligence and the most effective intelligence comes from those who are closest to the action. In our schools, the person closest to the action is the student—the individual who is the recipient of our service delivery. How do we know if the student finds a book to be bland and uninteresting? Do we know if the student feels safe? Can we tell if a student is being bullied? Is the new math software user-friendly? Do students like the food in the cafeteria? What teachers intimidate students? If we are curious about the answers to these questions, we must seek input from students. Not surprisingly, we have found that students are eager to share their thoughts about the organization, policies, teachers, parking, school lunches, course work, and many other areas of interest.

A common way of gathering information from students is to survey them and this we do. Surveys, however, have limitations. A survey does not allow for a two-way conversation to explore the depth and breadth of issues. Nor does a survey create opportunities to involve the respondent in finding and carrying out solutions to the problems that may be identified. Seeking another way to gather high quality information from students and to put this information to use, we decided to create an advisory council populated by the high school student council presidents. This council would be organized and facilitated by the superintendent and senior district administrators who would make it a point to regularly attend the council meetings.

As it turned out, we only needed to convene the council; the students took care of coordinating the council, selecting their council officers, and creating their own meeting agendas. All we had to do was follow their lead. The superintendent and district administrators met with the council every two months at an agreed upon location and the students met among themselves on the off month, rotating their meetings among each high school. They showed up on time, they came ready for work, and we never had trouble from any of the students. Admittedly, as student council presidents, these students had already been recognized as leaders by their peers, but we wondered if they would have the maturity to function as leaders with administrators. Absolutely! And, it cost the school district next to nothing to get this talent, time, and commitment—we paid for their participation by giving them access to the refrigerator. It's amazing how important food is to the teenager! When they met in the schools, they figured out how to get the hosting school staff to buy them pizza. They're not only good leaders; they're refreshingly smart.

During the meetings, the students were very productive. Being recognized as leaders in their own schools, these students were seldom inhibited at the advisory council meetings and were willing to share their thoughts on any subject. For instance, using this process, students brought to our attention their concerns about the district's dress code. Reportedly, one student had been talking about his math teacher and her style of dress, which he deemed unprofessional, and then the others chimed in with their opinions. When these students brought this issue to our joint meeting, we met their questions with questions of our own. Do all teachers dress this way? What do you think is proper dress? Why is this a problem for you? What needs to be done to solve it? From the discussion of how teachers dressed, we moved to how students dressed and they were very animated about this topic as well. Imagine the discussion about sagging pants, bare midriffs, spaghetti straps, and the like. Intense discussions took place over several months. Students were given homework to research other district dress code policies and consider how the community would be made aware of a dress code policy. They were asked to describe how a policy would be implemented and how the policy could be enforced.

As we began to formulate our ideas on dress codes for staff and students, we, the adults, worried about a problem of a different nature. When the time came to take this issue to the board of education, how would they react when we prefaced our comments by saying that it was the students who first brought this issue to our attention? As it turned out, we need not have worried; the board was very supportive and wanted to tighten up the dress code standards even more than the students did—no surprise there. While educators will hold many different opinions on dress code policies, whether for students or staff, the point that we are making with this example is that it was our students who were first empowered to explore this issue and it was our students who helped to implement the policy when it was eventually adopted by the board. This is how the best businesses in the world do so well—listening to and understanding their customers.

For the superintendent, meeting with students was always energizing, to see the talents and enthusiasm that they brought to the table and to witness their commitment to their schools, peers, and community. Yes, superintendents could get stretched pretty thin with one more group that requires their attention. But what superintendent can say no to an opportunity to get this kind of help from our chief stakeholder? A big advantage educators have over business is the ability of their students (the "products," so to speak) to talk to them and make suggestions on how their educational experience (the "manufacturing process," so to speak) can be improved. Are you taking advantage of that input?

Support Services Staff

Because all students matter, we must be careful not to become too narrowly focused on academics; we need to ensure that we address students' social-emotional concerns as well, including issues such as bullying, drugs, alcohol, sex, peer pressures, and family concerns. Thankfully, many of our students navigate concerns like these with minimal need of assistance; however, a significant number of our students need help with more than reading, writing, and arithmetic. In part, we create some of these social-emotional problems ourselves. With higher standards for achievement, we can expect a corresponding rise in test anxiety and corollary problems associated with school failure.

On top of pressures to achieve in school and gain peer acceptance, remember too that our students are often in ballet, band, French club, sports, or working after school. By comparison, our lives as adults are relatively simple. Sometimes, the hectic lives of our students would come to the superintendent's attention when parents requested school transfers, thinking that the problems their child was experiencing were with the teachers or peers at the school. Discussion with the parents would sometimes reveal enormous pressures on the child trying to maintain high grades, a full schedule of school and community activities, and responsibilities at home as well. These can all exact a toll on our students.

If all students matter, we need to provide a variety of support services such as school counselors, psychologists, social workers, nurses, and the like. And, even with these roles in place, we must guard against compartmentalizing the roles. All staff in the building have to perform in the role of "counselor," "psychologist," "social worker," or "nurse." What caring teacher has not helped comfort a student with a skinned knee or wounded pride? What caring teacher has not interceded on behalf of the student who is on the outside looking in? When we talk counseling, we're not just thinking of the guidance counselor. We're also thinking of teachers, coaches, cafeteria staff, and volunteers all playing a role. If all students matter, then every child should know that at least one caring adult on campus holds a special spot in his or her heart and mind for him or her.

This focus on the whole person is no different in the business world. Successful businesses have figured out how important it is to focus on the whole person. At work, adults are more productive when they know that their business will accommodate home and family concerns. Morale is better, attendance is better, productivity is better. Similarly, students will be more successful when they know that school is a home away from home.

Despite the argument we have advanced, some in the public will still question why we need counseling and associated support services. After all, at their place of work, there is probably not a counselor with whom they can talk; instead, the business may provide some insurance coverage for counseling. There may not be a nurse who can dispense medicine for the cold they contacted. Instead, the business may have a sick day policy and the employee will need to make an appointment with a doctor. However, unlike a business where the product of the business is something that employees produce, in schools our "product" is the student. To use business-like terminology, in education, we must ensure that our product is healthy and functioning at optimal efficiency so that we can have a maximum impact on the product—teach the student to read, write, and calculate. Businesses seek to control their raw materials, better ensuring their final product will be of the highest quality. Similarly, educators want our students to be well cared for, better ensuring our ability to teach them.

It could even be argued that it is not the school's mission to feed students; however, a student who goes without lunch will not learn well in the afternoon. Similarly, a student who has unattended social-emotional needs will not learn well. For instance, it has been well documented that school nursing services make it possible for students to stay in school, or if out sick, to return to school sooner. Moreover, nurses in our schools treat student illnesses, relieving teachers of that burden. The school nurse, counselor, social worker, and psychologist all allow the teacher to cover more academic ground and help to support the student in the classroom.

In education, our business is the whole child. We recognize that this approach is different from most businesses. Except for the unusual business, the social-emotional needs of employees are typically handled outside the work environment. In fact, issues such as drug use and alcoholism could result in unemployment. True, we will suspend students for similar offenses for a number of days or longer periods, and in very few cases expel them, but generally speaking, we don't want to expel students like a business might let employees go. More than anyone else, educators appreciate that every student who drops out or fails to learn to read is a failure of public education and a problem for the community. Although we know that we will have our failures, we don't like it and because education is first and foremost a relationship between teacher and student, we take this failure personally.

We accept that our primary mission is to educate children to read, write, and calculate (along with all the other subjects) and we know that support services are essential to our carrying out this mission. The counselor, psychologist, social worker, school nurse, and others are essential to this mission. To the extent that we can align these specialties with the educational mission, then we will better achieve our goal of educating all students to their potential.

WHAT YOU CAN DO TO IMPROVE

- Convene a healthy school task force to compare and contrast your schools on student demographic, achievement, and social-emotional variables
- Infuse character education throughout the instructional curriculum
- Form a superintendent's student council
- Include support service staff in decision-making processes regarding major educational initiatives

---

TEACHERS MATTER MOST

Businesses are what their employees make them. Yes, a competent leader is very important, but without high quality employees the business will never achieve excellence. The same is true for schools and teachers. In education as in business, there are many things that contribute to great employees—more than just pay and benefits. Having leaders who care about their employees is often cited by teachers as one of the top factors motivating their performance. Your success as a leader will be dependent in large measure on how well you take care of your teachers.

Working With Teachers' Organizations

We are all familiar with research literature that highlights the importance of the classroom teacher. For those of us who have long been in the business of public education, this is a no-brainer. Among the variables that are in the control of our schools, the classroom teacher is the most important variable contributing to students' academic success. Yes, research also tells us that principals are important to student success, but what is a principal without great teachers? Quality teachers challenge students to excel, provide lessons that are at the level that students can succeed, and go above and beyond the class period in their efforts to meet the needs of all students. As a leader at the school, the principal's task is to create the working conditions that will support and promote great teaching.

Successful schools and school districts will recognize the importance of providing teachers with a positive working environment. In North Carolina, findings reported for the Governor's Teacher Working Conditions survey consistently reveal that one of the top concerns that teachers express is their need to work in a positive and supportive working environment. (The Governor's Teacher Working Conditions Survey can be found at http://www.northcarolinatwc.org/.) Teachers who feel respected and supported will stay longer in your organization, have fewer absences during the year, and exhibit a higher degree of professional involvement—all factors that will manifest in higher achievement for students.

Leaders who expect to have quality teachers will provide these teachers with the respect and support they deserve. To provide that support and create a positive working environment, school principals must listen to teachers and act on their concerns. Principals know this, but it is equally important for superintendents to listen to the voices representing teacher organizations. The superintendent may expect that teachers will organize at the local level to represent their own professional interests, whether this be the school or the school district. Will the superintendent's relationship with the teacher organization be adversarial or collaborative?

Teacher organizations take many forms across the nation; in some states they are organized as unions with powers to represent teachers in salary negotiations, and in some states as associations with less legal power but no less moral and persuasive authority. North Carolina does not have teachers' unions but does have associations. The North Carolina Association of Educators (NCAE) functions as both an advocate and lobbyist for teacher's rights. NCAE's advocacy focuses on providing teacher-training programs designed to inform teachers about their rights and direct them to resources that will help improve their techniques in the classroom. Much of the training NCAE provides teachers is in the area of helping them know their rights when they're evaluated, where to go or whom to approach to find answers to their questions, and getting their needs met if they should be deemed an unsatisfactory teacher. NCAE is also a determined lobbyist for improving teacher working conditions, including providing teacher mentors and better salaries.

Recognizing the importance of collaborating with our teachers, in Wake County we made the local NCAE unit a full member of the superintendent's administrative cabinet. An NCAE representative met every week with the top leaders in the school district to discuss the pertinent issues of the day in a free and open exchange.

Prior to having an NCAE representative at the cabinet table, there was a great deal of animosity between teachers and school district administrators, which could be seen in the tug of war over issues such as duty-free lunch, planning periods, new programs such as block scheduling, and other expectations of teachers including extra-duty and cocurricular responsibilities. In the days before being extended an invitation to join the superintendent's cabinet, NCAE representatives would formulate a series of questions from their organization for school district administrators to answer. Those answers, as well as the questions, were published in the NCAE monthly newsletter. Somehow, we could never satisfactorily answer the questions; it seemed that one answer only led to more questions and miscommunications would often turn on a phrase or single word.

Since sending a representative to join the superintendent's weekly cabinet meetings, the monthly question and answer scenario has been completely eliminated. NCAE is able to ask their questions at the cabinet meetings and subsequently provide answers to their membership through their own regular meetings. The NCAE representative carries this information back to the teacher membership personally, rather than the impersonal question/answer communication via newsletter. An added benefit of this form of communication is that the NCAE representative is able to address teacher questions in greater detail.

Coming to the cabinet meeting also helped to establish stronger relationships between the teacher organization and district administrators. Now, NCAE leaders will pick up the phone and call an administrator when there is a question rather than jumping to a conclusion that may be false or incomplete. It is amazing how many times we would get a call about a developing issue and, without waiting for the next cabinet meeting, we were able to respond by going to the NCAE organization, addressing the issue in that forum, and being present to field questions. This relationship building is a two-way street as district administrators are now more comfortable with picking up the phone and calling NCAE representatives to discuss concerns and issues.

One example of an issue where having NCAE at the cabinet meeting made an important difference was block scheduling. The school district had tried to introduce block scheduling in a number of individual high schools, one school at a time, but had been unable to make any progress. When block scheduling was attempted one school at a time, we had meltdown at each school. Teachers at each school expressed too many issues and we had too little time to respond to all concerns. Block scheduling had been seen as something sinister, even anti-teacher, because of how it would require changes in teaching methodology, lesson plans, and ultimately the structure of a high school. And yet, we were confident that block scheduling was something we needed to do for the academic success of our students. For us, the most important consideration was the additional flexibility that block scheduling would permit, allowing schools to provide more course selection and increased variety of courses for all students—advanced and at-risk.

With an NCAE representative at the cabinet meetings, we adopted a different strategy. Rather than one school at a time, we determined that we would first work out the significant issues in a collaborative partnership with the NCAE organization. Through collaboration with NCAE, the strategy was to have teachers and principals solidly on board, after which we would then approach the school board and the community. Before going to the school board, we wanted to be sure that the teachers and school administrators would join together to say, "We can make this work." In time, as this discussion played out at the weekly cabinet meetings, the NCAE organization joined with the school district administration to put out information about block scheduling and address the why, how, when, and what questions about the block scheduling initiative. Subsequently, when we took this issue to the school board, we got a unanimous vote.

Naturally, superintendents should proceed cautiously if they want to bring the teacher organization into a full partnership with their school districts. If this approach is new, one should appreciate that the relationship is fragile in the early stage. Trust is key to any relationship and this is true in a relationship between a school district and the teachers' organization. While the relationship is building, a superintendent needs to be careful about how much is revealed—possibly putting less challenging issues on the table until the relationship grows stronger, when more challenging issues can be entertained in an open dialogue. When we first invited NCAE to the superintendent's cabinet, we would share information about the district as a whole and some of the major decisions that we were planning to make, but this information didn't fall into the critical category. This was also a learning and trust-building experience for the district administrators at the cabinet meeting. Cabinet administrators initially responded with some degree of suspicion, but the relationship grew over time.

In Wake County, teachers strive to excel. Knowing that they are represented at the highest levels of the school district is undoubtedly one of the reasons why Wake County teachers often go above and beyond the call of duty.

Relative to the premise of this book, a quality business principle that is at work in this approach is bringing all stakeholders under the tent, involving all in the decision-making process. Rather than being a top-down organization, successful businesses make certain all the voices are heard. Also, from a systems perspective, this approach is one that reduces artificial boundaries that can be barriers to collaborative partnerships. Before NCAE joined the superintendent's cabinet, there was a rather fixed boundary between the two organizations with the chief vehicle for communication being through the written questions and answers. After joining the cabinet, this boundary began to dissolve—to become more permeable and allow for a greater flow of information, ideas, and working relations. Both organizations retained their identities and both strove to represent their professional interests, while both organizations also knew that we were in a working relationship for the common good of students.

Superintendent's Teacher Advisory Council

How much do we care about our teachers; is it enough that we will work to improve their working conditions? We know based on our observations of human beings and scientific research that people respond favorably to positive reinforcement. In North Carolina, the Teacher Working Conditions Survey lists adverse working conditions as one of the significant reasons that teachers choose to leave the profession. For teachers, "working conditions" is typically their way of saying whether they feel supported by their principal and others in the hierarchy. This support for teachers and teaching comes in a number of forms such as adequate supplies and materials, decision-making empowerment, a nurturing work environment, support with student discipline, fair and equitable treatment, recognition for achievements, etc. Teachers who are supported in these ways are usually much happier and are less likely to leave their school or profession.

Teachers are eager to share their thoughts about teaching and all the factors that impact their working conditions. They know first hand what is working well instructionally and how best to improve the profession. In Wake County, an approach that was valuable in getting good information about ways and means of improving teachers' working conditions was the creation of a Superintendent's Teacher Advisory Council (STAC). The idea behind STAC was simple—to ask teachers what they thought on a variety of issues affecting their professional lives. STAC was created after a series of teacher forums around the district, where teachers from over seventy different schools voiced their concerns about working conditions relative to testing, salary, student discipline, respect, training, supplies and equipment, and many other issues.

Teachers applied to participate on STAC, with the application requiring full-time teachers who had at least three years of experience. They also needed their principal's approval. Participants were told that they could expect at least six meetings, each half a day, spread evenly across the year, and participate for two-year terms. Additionally, classroom substitutes would be provided for the teachers. Applications were sent to a screening committee, which chose applicants by grade level, geography, race, gender, and subject area to ensure a diversity of perspectives. The final number of STAC members consisted of eighteen to twenty teachers representing the spectrum of teachers in the school system. For our meetings, a neutral facilitator was provided to keep the meetings focused and outcome specific.

Not surprisingly, STAC participants were representative of the district's teacher leadership. We know that teachers are constantly emerging as leaders in their schools and communities and seek outlets through which they can express this leadership. However, these risk takers too often find themselves isolated and not able to satisfy their desire to connect with other educators who are taking risks, being innovative, and accepting leadership challenges. Think of the possibilities if we are able to facilitate this leadership experience for teachers and harness the power of their ideas. We would see the skill and experience of some of the master teachers taking center stage. Showing pride in their work, these teachers would define a good classroom and/or a good school and would work alongside administration to engage the public to answer the question, "How are our schools doing?" Being recognized for their leadership, we would expect that the sense of accomplishment would be a major factor in these teachers' decisions to continue in the teaching profession.

Once organized, STAC was empowered to take on tough issues but couldn't just complain and say it was someone else's issue. STAC members were expected to find solutions in concert with the administration. Consequently, subcommittees were created to delve deeper into an issue. Their job was to make decisions after finding the best research and data to support their solutions. Magic was generated when lateral entry, veterans, special education, coaches, and other teaching specialists collectively tackled an issue. These teacher leaders found innovative means to keep current on educational issues and sought to understand those issues from the context of others' perspectives, which extended their understanding to the broader educational context where policies are developed.

A retreat was held for the STAC members to allow them to spend quality time together and focus attention on developing teacher leadership in Wake County. Subsequently, after a number of work sessions, the teacher advisory council adopted the following vision: *To be a change agent for effective schools*, and mission statement: *To foster teacher leadership in Wake County*. To support STAC's mission, the advisory council agreed to the following goals:

- To design and develop an intentional and vibrant WCPSS teacher leadership system
- To create a community awareness campaign to transform Wake County's public perception of teachers and teaching
- To support WCPSS in the creation/implementation of a strategic pathway for teacher development, enhancement, and compensation

Through working on the STAC goals, our collaborative hope was to elevate the profession of teachers within and beyond Wake County. The advisory council has proved to be extremely valuable in this regard, providing first-hand insight into the current lives and needs of our teachers, and has helped the school administration stay focused and grounded on STAC's goals. STAC members generally became our eyes and ears for the teachers and often defended us when they knew the administration was being falsely accused. With membership on STAC rotating every two years, the cadre of teachers who gain this experience working alongside the administration continues to grow in the district.

STAC is one means for administrators to collect feedback that is truly focused on continuous improvement—and this feedback isn't always pleasant to hear. Listening to our teachers has proven to be the key to success with STAC, and working together with our teachers to make a difference is a constant source of renewal for our administrators.

The Culture of Quality

Business leaders understand that the employee is a key factor contributing to productivity. While businesses typically deal with a product, in the school "business," we're dealing with children, and must be careful not to draw too many parallels. Many of the factors that teacher employees bring to bear on the "product" are difficult to quantify, such as the heart that we say is an important component of the teacher/student relationship. Generally, teachers' content knowledge, classroom management, and interpersonal connections that they make with their students will define quality teachers.

Acquiring and sustaining quality in these areas requires leaders to seek out teachers who are never satisfied with their knowledge base and are in a constant state of self-renewal. These are the teachers who will spend considerable hours involved in staff development, reading new material, seeking best practices based on empirical research, and studying the fundamentals of child development. These teachers know there is no set template to follow, as each child is different and has a different set of needs. In essence, a quality teacher is one who never stops learning, who can individualize instruction, and who cares passionately that every single child "gets it."

Like the chicken and the egg question, we can ask which comes first—the quality teacher, the quality principal, the quality superintendent, or the school culture. And, like the chicken and the egg, the answer is that they all matter. Still, if you're the school's leader, you must start somewhere, and we suggest this should be school culture. When superintendents visit schools to meet with their principals, will all the personnel and accouterments that surround the superintendent project a culture of achievement? Similarly, when the principal visits teachers, will their classrooms project a culture of achievement? Developing a culture takes time; consistency and stability in leadership are important and, once established, the culture can in turn support the development of the next leader. Whoever follows the superintendent or principal will be impacted by the culture.

In the creation of culture, the role of the superintendent is to visualize and verbalize the mission and goals of the school district. To the extent that the superintendent is passionate about instruction and champions the right of every child to be challenged academically, then those principals who are hired to run the schools will model the superintendent. In the schools, this culture of achievement is driven by the principal who believes the road to excellence is with every child being challenged and expected to work to his or her potential. Therefore, part of the answer to creating a strong school culture lies in the superintendent's vision and capable principals who will share this vision, who understand instruction, who are driven to challenge every child, and who know that teachers matter most. In Wake County, there are many schools where any prospective teaching candidate, upon entering the building, will know that student achievement is central to the school's culture—work products in the hallways speak of this culture, the demeanor of teachers toward their students speak of this culture, and even the conversation in the teachers' lounge speaks of this culture. To quantify these intangibles is difficult, but they tell a story. Every administrator and teacher knows a quality school when they walk into one.

In the school, a culture of high expectations is about teachers feeling and being empowered. The successful principal insists that teachers take ownership for student instruction and learning. In matters of budget, a quality principal will find ways to make things happen for teachers through prioritizing and deciding with teachers what is important. One powerful, yet inexpensive, way to impact culture is to support the development of professional learning communities among the school's teachers.

Professional learning communities have gained much attention in the recent educational literature; however, there is little that is new about these arrangements. Quality teachers have always found ways to engage each other, share information on best practices, and support each other in challenging circumstances. If anything, what may be new about professional learning communities is how the school leadership is awakening to the need to create the infrastructure that will allow teachers to collaborate in a consistent and organized fashion. The leadership must create the opportunities for teachers to work together to ask fundamental questions and seek solutions. Working as a team seeking answers to how to motivate and help all students achieve, the teachers become the driving force in the school's instructional program and define the culture of achievement at the school. This level of ownership almost always guarantees a high level of student success.

For those in administration, central office, and schools, an issue becomes how to support our teachers when they do identify needs and solutions. In fiscal matters, the successful principal or superintendent will strive to realign the budget to accommodate the needs of empowering teachers, realizing that this is a zero sum game. If something new is to be provided, something else must go. How about creating planning time? If teachers are going to be asking and answering key questions as a team, they need team planning time in the school day to do this. What about professional development? Teachers need access to high quality, ongoing professional development. Moreover, as the needs of children change, so too will teachers' training needs change, or as teachers become accomplished with one level of professional development, then they must be challenged to seek another level—always learning.

In the past, we believed once teachers received their university degrees, they could simply go out and teach. Teachers were thrust into classrooms and were expected to teach. Any additional staff development they received was usually in the summer and, in some cases, had little to do with their needs and more to do with keeping their certificate updated. Teachers would typically sign up for staff development if they expected to enjoy it, but the program may have had little to do with improving their performance in the classroom. In contrast to this old style of doing business, we now know that professional development must be continuous, support lifelong learning, and be designed to align with the goals and needs of the school's instructional program.

The professional learning community of the twenty-first century looks very directly at the teachers' needs as these relate to their students' needs. In the past, professional development might not have been well aligned to training teachers to meet student needs. Today, this training will differ every year and it must be available when needed, embedded in the teacher's day and curriculum, and conducted by highly skilled trainers. Trainers must be able to give the teachers personal examples, demonstrate the examples, and be willing to follow up with the teacher in a live classroom situation akin to the "master" teacher model.

When well organized and supported, the professional learning community among teachers provides participating teachers with informal feedback on their practices and performance. Separate from but no less important than this informal feedback among colleagues, the principal's formal evaluation of each teacher is another means of advancing the school's culture of achievement. As in business, the formal evaluation must be more than a perfunctory exercise, and must incorporate feedback in the form of classroom observation, student observations, parent observations, peer observations, and the teacher's own self-assessment—all pieces are necessary. The most readily apparent aspect of the formal evaluation is when the principal visits the classroom. Sometimes the visits are announced and sometimes unannounced and the purpose is to observe the teacher in action and determine if good instructional practices are used, respect for the students is evident, and the students are learning at a rate commensurate with success. To carry out this assessment, the principal needs to have an understanding of pedagogy, classroom management, and the fundamentals of teaching and learning. Putting it bluntly, the principal should be able to assume the teacher's place in the classroom and be ready to demonstrate quality teaching. If you're not this kind of leader, then how can you evaluate, much less advise, a teacher on these qualities? Areas such as content knowledge, time on task, student management, classroom mobility, comprehensive lesson plans, appropriate tools and equipment for success, and unique ability to deliver the lesson all play a part in how well the teacher performs. The principal needs to be the master of these competencies as well.

The day of judging teachers by how well they manage student behavior is long past. While classroom management will always be a necessary skill, student achievement is now the mantra, and accountability models exist for judging teachers and schools in regards to how well their students are learning. The thinking is that if students are engaged in the learning process, then classroom management becomes less of a concern.

The most enjoyable aspect of superintendents' work should be when they get the chance to visit classrooms and meet the teachers and students. When the day is too busy to permit this and the weeks fly by, even visiting a school and classroom in the evening can be a reflective and rewarding time. Entering the school and classrooms and just looking about provides a flavor for the culture of achievement that is present.

WHAT YOU CAN DO TO IMPROVE

- Put the teacher's union representative on the superintendent's cabinet
- Survey your teachers about their satisfaction with their jobs and working conditions
- Form a superintendent's teacher advisory council
- Get to know your teachers when you visit the schools

PARENTS MATTER MOST

To business people, who typically begin with the end in sight, nothing is more important than a satisfied customer, and businesses will devote time and money trying to measure that satisfaction. Likewise, educational leaders want satisfied parents and it behooves the leader to have a "marketing and public relations" program to reach out to parents. If the superintendent or principal waits for parents to contact them, much of what they will hear will likely be complaints. However, if the superintendent and principal initiate the contact, seeking to actively engage parents in an ongoing conversation, then it is more likely that they will get useful information. Whether in business or education, communication is the key to satisfied customers.

Informing the Public About Educational Success

With respect to educating our nation's children and youth, school and home must become inseparable and indistinguishable from each other. Just as we must open our schools to parents and the community—invite them to come in and work alongside us—so too we must ensure that the homes in our community are infused with education and education-speak. We need everyone to be in the same book reading the same page about educational excellence. We must tell our story and tell it well.

One of the significant differences between business management and K–12 educators is our tendency to not be proactive about tooting our own horn. We don't do that very well. While there are thousands of success stories every day, we often allow the media to dictate which stories will be written, viewed, or heard on the radio—as if we have no control over engaging our consumers. In fact, we have tremendous control and power to get our message out. Students, for one example, can be our ambassadors and carry the message to our parents.

Students can take a newsletter home that regularly talks about the issues, goals, and mission of the school district and pertinent topics for parents. When we were knee-deep in the issue of student assignment while also building the case for our bond referendum, we created a newsletter called "Growth Matters." It was a regular newsletter that we sent home via students to update parents about growth, the impact of growth on instruction and facilities, where in the county we were growing more rapidly, and the demographic makeup of the growth. Subsequently, it was not news to our parents when they read in the newspaper that Wake County was growing significantly; they had been receiving that information regularly from us. The same information was being shared with staff through a newsletter called "Education Matters." Between these two publications, we kept our parent community and staff informed. They could talk intelligently about growth using data that were current and could refute arguments of our detractors simply because they were informed. We believe the success of the 2006 bond referendum had its roots in this information.

Many of our success stories centered around achieving the 95 percent goal. We wanted to make certain that schools and teachers were highlighted for the tremendous work they had accomplished in pursuit of this goal. To accomplish this, we used successful schools as models. Many of our schools win national awards and we made sure this was well publicized with our parents. For instance, people in the district and throughout North Carolina are familiar with Lockhart Elementary School—and not by accident. By design, we gave this school a sort of celebrity status. Lockhart was a school with few resources, yet they achieved a 95 percent proficiency rate. Through newsletters and presentations, we highlighted their Accelerated Learning Program, designed to provide tutoring and remediation for students throughout the year to get them on track earlier.

WCPSS is also recognized nationwide for its magnet schools program, and we tout the district's magnet programs every time the Magnet Schools of America Association recognizes our magnet schools with an award. We publish these schools in our parent newsletters, recognize them at school board meetings, and we send personal e-mails to staff at those schools praising them. We also attend the schools' celebratory assemblies for staff, students, and parents.

Also, honoring our students and parents, every month at school board meetings, we shine the spotlight on students. We believe that all board sessions go better when we are reminded that our mission is to educate children. "Spotlight on Students" provides this reminder. Each month, we bring in student representatives from a collection of schools—every school has opportunities to participate using criteria such as academic growth, strong character, most improved, and/or able to overcome significant obstacles (health or otherwise). The district has been doing "Spotlight on Students" for at least fifteen years, and it is still a well-loved program, especially by the students who have their family members and school staff in the audience. And because these meetings are broadcast on local cable channels, many of the students we highlight earn a measure of celebrity status back at their school and in their neighborhood. The Spotlight on Students program provides opportunities to publicly praise our hard-working students in front of their proud parents who also appreciate the recognition of being associated with these successful students.

Student Assignment

We have made the point that it is necessary to involve all stakeholders in your communications and decision-making processes. In this regard, we have said that students matter most. We have also said that teachers matter most. And now, we say that parents matter most. But really, you might ask, who matters the most? Well, they all do. Give any of these audiences the short shrift at your peril. A tenet of modern-day business best practices is excellence in communications of all kinds, from employees to customers to the public. Parents are a major part of your public, ready to praise or criticize at any moment.

In Wake County, the most contentious issue for parents is probably the district's practice of making student assignments. The district has an extensive network of magnet schools that provides a variety of voluntary choices for parents, but the district otherwise assigns students to schools based on a number of factors. Proximity to the school is a major factor and most schools will have base "nodes" (similar to zip code zones, but much smaller) in close proximity to the school that are assigned to each school. Students in a particular base node know which school they are to attend, except for those who may be accepted into magnet schools. However, the base nodes are sometimes assigned to schools more distant than the nearest neighborhood school, based on the school district's effort to maintain a diverse enrollment at all of its schools. With regard to diversity, the percentage of low-income students living within a particular base node and/or the percentage of students in that node not achieving at grade level are two factors the district will consider when assigning the node to a particular school.

Also, the ceaseless growth in student enrollment that the district has been experiencing for the past twenty years, with the attendant need to build and populate new schools, creates situations where it is deemed necessary to move a node from a crowded school and assign it to a newly opened school. For the last twenty years, population growth in the school district has ranged from 1 percent to 6 percent per year, translating into thousands of new students each year. For instance, in the 2004–05 year, the district grew by 6,439 students; in 2005–06, the district grew by 7,568 students.

The new schools that must be built to house these students will necessarily be populated largely with students from other existing schools, and many of these students will be drawn from existing schools that are overcrowded. To not do so would cause both the existing and new schools to operate less than effectively and efficiently. New schools would not be fully utilized for a number of years, and the existing overcrowded schools suffer from too few classrooms, crowded hallways, increased disciplinary problems, lunches beginning at 10:00 a.m., and other problems, including increased wear and tear on the facilities. Thus, there is a major effort to keep all schools at a healthy level of student population. Everyone likes this idea *except* parents whose children are relocated—they want other children to be relocated.

Unquestionably, the assignment of students to schools is a challenging task for the district administration and board of education, and sometimes an unpleasant experience for parents. Thousands of students are reassigned in most years. Many parents take this in stride and quickly adjust, but some parents resist reassignment by all means, including legal.

For many years, the Wake County Board of Education handled reassignment in a way that made sense to them. The school administration would convene a committee of supportive parents from all over the county, explain in detail the problems faced, and ask their advice and input on how to make the reassignments with the least angst. This input was gathered over several months and the administration would present the plan to the board of education and public in late January. The board would hold public hearings and work sessions in February and vote in March. Although there were public hearings, much of the work in devising the plan had been done with very little parent input.

As soon as the administration's plan was reported to the board, those parents whose children were slated for reassignment started lobbying school board members to move someone else and leave them alone. The lobbying was passionate and relentless. Sometimes it worked and the board would revise the plan, giving hope and reinforcement to future groups to do the same thing. This process exhausted everyone—the parents (whether or not they were successful), the school board members who were taking hundreds of phone calls and working long sessions, and the school administrators who would have to defend their recommendations and then sometimes undo them for even worse choices.

In 2001, WCPSS tried another system we modeled upon the North Carolina Department of Transportation (DOT). Every state has a DOT or something similar with the job to build and maintain roads throughout its state. For DOT, the most difficult aspect of this task may not be the building of a brand new road, but getting the public to believe that the best path has been chosen. After all, some people don't want roads in their backyards, while others want the road to pass by their business. In North Carolina and other states, the DOT methodology is to present for public comment several alternatives, take feedback, digest it, and then go out with a proposal that has been changed due to the public input. The proposal that is ultimately presented is prepared only after the public has had numerous opportunities for input. Along with securing extensive public input, repeating this practice again and again, year after year, accomplishes other objectives including helping citizens to understand the problems of building roads, affording them opportunities to voice their opinions, and getting all used to the idea that each person may not get what each wants. This approach requires advance work; the process must start long before any pavement is laid down.

In 2001, the school district started public hearings for the next year's assignment plan in August when school started. Meetings were held at a number of sites around the county, input was received, and ideas were developed. Two months later, more meetings were held with specific reassignments suggested. More input was received and changes were made. Six weeks later, a revised plan was released and more input taken. By the time the administration's proposal was presented to the board in early February, there were no surprises. Everyone who would be impacted had had plenty of notice and plenty of time to give their input.

As a result of this more lengthy planning process, the parents were less angry. True, the board of education members still received lobbying phone calls, but far fewer, and the public hearings that followed the administration's presentation of the proposal had fewer in attendance—most people had already had their say. The district administration had received valuable and constructive input in a much less stressful manner and there was a greater belief in the community that the final product was the best that could be done.

In 2005, almost 11,000 students were reassigned due to the high growth and severe overcrowding, and the new student assignment method yielded a more satisfied customer. Sure, there remained those who were not satisfied—this would be expected with 11,000 reassignments—but on whole, the process of involving the community served the district well. Although change is often upsetting, the process the school district is now following allows for greater parent input through frequent meetings as well as Internet communications. This input is distilled and refined in an iterative process to produce the most satisfactory plan—a plan that maintains healthy schools throughout the school district and utilizes the capacity of all schools, providing good stewardship of the public's trust and money. Until district enrollment growth stabilizes, the school district will always be challenged with balancing the enrollment and maintenance of existing schools with populating new schools and keeping all schools healthy. Now, if only our DOT could just build roads as cost efficiently as we educate our children!

Role of the PTA Council

When defining key stakeholders of any school district, one group is especially important to the district's success and that is the parents' organization. In Wake County, we call this group the Parent-Teachers Association (PTA). In every school, supportive parents care deeply about their child's school. Through their volunteer activities and time spent on campus, these parents gain unique insight into the inner workings of the local school and school district. They see how teachers interact with the students; they see if every student has a textbook; they see how well the cafeteria is being operated. Also, remember that many of these parents have children in more than one school and they are able to compare and contrast how different schools operate.

When properly cultivated and supported, these parents can be a unique band of foot soldiers for the district. Think of a small cluster of strong supporters in every school carrying the message of the district to other parents and nonparents alike. Note that we said, "properly cultivated and supported," meaning that the top-level leadership in the district is responsible to help make the PTA one of the strongest organizations in the school. This means attending PTA meetings, championing their projects, and meeting with their leadership on a regular basis. In fact, we believe the PTA organizations are so important that we made it possible for the county's PTA leadership to meet with our administrative cabinet monthly. Moreover, we complemented this monthly forum by establishing a superintendent's Parents' Advisory Council—a diverse group of parents representing geography, grade level, race, and gender. The Parents' Advisory Council met with the superintendent for half a day, five to six times a year, to address pertinent issues the district faced.

The feedback we received from parents chosen for this council told us that they greatly valued the opportunity to get more in-depth information about the school system and for their voices to be heard and become part of the solutions. Imagine the situation in a school district where there is an adversarial relationship between the administration and the parents' organization—not at all good, if only because technology now allows disgruntled parents to readily reach an army of other parents who can easily become sympathizers and detractors. A band of supporters can turn on you almost overnight and become an army of detractors.

PTAs often have a goal at the school level to have 100 percent of their students represented in their parent membership. This is especially true at the elementary grades. The PTA membership numbers can be bolstered when parents feel their volunteer time and effort are used appropriately and when the school administration shows respect to the PTA. PTA members appreciate being rewarded and recognized through formal activities spearheaded by the superintendent and school board. For instance, we have noted how very grateful parents are when they're recognized for their work at a regular school board meeting. Like our children, our parents too like to feel needed and appreciated, and know that their work makes a difference in the life of a child—their own children and others. When we're able to support our parents in this way, they will give freely of their time.

One-to-One With Parents

Occasionally, the superintendent must meet with individual parents, even in the largest of school districts. We have a process in place that requires parents to begin at the lowest level where their concern originated, for instance, with the classroom teacher. If their concern is not satisfied at that level, then they may take their concern to the school principal, then the area assistant administrator for that school, and eventually the superintendent. Our experience has been that 99.9 percent of the problems will be—and in fact, should be—solved before reaching the superintendent. However, the 0.1 percent of problems that do find their way to the superintendent's desk will represent some of the toughest issues for the superintendent. To make matters even more challenging, often the dissenting parent in these cases has the support of another parent advocate, somebody who is well read, articulate, has done the homework, has followed the process, and has decided that the parent should not accept "No" for an answer. Whether the parent alone or the parent with an advocate, some will not be satisfied until they reach the very top. (Many parents in these situations are prepared to take it to the "top"—or, as they put it, "All the way to the Supreme Court!") As superintendent, you will need to do your homework, research the issues, know the intricacies of what happened at the other levels, and determine whether there will be some way you can resolve the parent's concerns. And yes, in some instances, you can make an executive decision and resolve the issue to the parent's liking.

Superintendents who overturn an earlier decision and support the parent's request must let staff members know why they have chosen this route and reinforce their understanding with the staff that they didn't do anything wrong. There needs to be an appreciation that everyone is trying to do their job, as well as an understanding that bureaucracies can sometimes be unresponsive. These solitary decisions by superintendents on a parent's or child's behalf can have much larger impact on the school district, possibly revealing policies or processes that need improvements.

Typically, if you're forthright with parents and staff, most situations can be resolved amicably, even when you have to say "No." The superintendent will gain in any event—gain in understanding of the parents' concerns, gain in understanding how well systems are working in the district, and gain an understanding of the impact of policy and procedures on students. If school district policy is at issue, the superintendent can't violate policy and will need to stand by previous decisions. If the policy needs improvement, a process exists for changing it.

Before leaving this piece on parents, we need to also mention e-mail and how important this tool is to your communication and relations with parents. A typical day for a superintendent in a large school district could be in the neighborhood of 200–250 e-mails, many from staff and many from the community. Despite this volume, it is a sound philosophy to always try to respond within the same day, whether this is via e-mail, voicemail, or snail mail. Certainly, this can sometimes be a "bridge too far," but the superintendent needs to believe in the ethics of the practice of giving people respect through responding to their communications. Most of the communications will require only short replies—"thanks," "good idea," "let's set up a meeting," and the like. Even with such short replies, we've found that staff and parents are thankful when you respond to them personally. Personal communication with your parents will make or break a leader. A twenty-four-hour turnaround for your messages is strongly encouraged.

WHAT YOU CAN DO TO IMPROVE

- Use your students as ambassadors to carry home news about the school district
- Organize a student recognition program at school board meetings and schedule this so that parents, family, and friends can attend
- Engage parents early and frequently in major decision-making processes, affording them an authentic opportunity to have input
- Establish a districtwide organization of school-based PTAs and involve this group in your decision-making processes
- Respond to your e-mails within twenty-four hours

INVOLVING THE ENTIRE VILLAGE

Why do businesses sometimes advertise themselves without mentioning their product? Why do they sponsor school sports, charity events, and community programs? Because building a successful company includes building a positive image throughout the market and not just selling more products. Business people reach out to their community in many ways to accomplish this. So too must superintendents and school leaders reach out to the community in their districts, energizing volunteers, visiting churches, talking with the media, communicating the message, etc. It is true that it takes an entire village to raise a child.

10,000 Children Below Grade Level

Even in a large school district with more than 100,000 students, 10,000 students is a significant number! In the late 1990s, this is the number of students we knew were not meeting the school district's minimum standard of performing at grade level in the core content domains of reading and/or mathematics. The enrollment of the average school district in our state at that time was approximately 6,000 students. We had more students below grade level than the average-sized school district in our state. When we took a closer look at these students, we found even more disturbing facts. A disproportionate number of the students were minority students, low-income students, and students with disabilities. We knew we had two problems: too many students not performing at grade level, and a disproportionate impact on some population subgroups.

Like any business, public schools have productivity goals. And, similar to business, those goals should be measurable. Many school districts will identify a collection of goals; however, as we have described, beginning in the 1998–99 school year, WCPSS in one bold move decided on a single goal—that 95 percent of students would be at or above grade level by the 2002–03 school year, giving us only five years to make the grade.

Many detractors said the goal was too ambitious, unrealistic, political in nature, a PR campaign, and would create significant morale problems for teachers and principals with the ultimate price being paid by the student. What's interesting about this goal is that the idea for the goal originated in the business community. A meeting involving key business leaders took place at Wake Medical Center. It was in this forum that the business committee, having read the research on reading, recommended that we have a goal that all third graders be proficient in reading. From this meeting, we developed a consensus for Goal 2003—that 95 percent of students in Grades 3 and 8 would be proficient in both reading and math by 2003. When presented to the board of education, the goal was adopted with very little modification.

One might ask, "If you're following a business model, why 95 percent, why not 100 percent?" Well, in business, you're striving for perfection with materials that have less variance. Businesses are usually able to exercise greater control over their raw materials—accepting only those that meet a minimum standard. However, in public education where we're dealing with people, we have little to no control over the students we accept. Unlike raw materials, students have much greater variance—different social backgrounds, languages, aptitudes—and we're bound to accept them all. Actually, that's the way we like it; we're public educators and we take all comers. We accept the challenge to educate every child and want the community to know this is our mission. Following the board's decision to support and implement Goal 2003, we began marketing the goal through community forums, newsletters, speaker's bureaus, point of view articles, radio engagements, and any other media available to us.

Goal 2003 forced several changes: We aligned our curriculum to achieve the goal; we reallocated line items in the budget to specifically address the goal; we provided more professional development for teachers and administrators; we increased our efforts to help parents understand their role if the goal was to be achieved; and we established an accelerated learning program to provide extra assistance with tutoring by our teachers. The accelerated learning program (ALP) was designed primarily for afterschool, weekends, and intercession breaks (when students in the district's year-round schools were out on three to four week breaks) so that it could be carried out in a timely manner during the school year. We were not satisfied with our traditional summer school program, which we viewed as being more of a punishment for students who didn't achieve during the school year and less an instructional program. We felt that summer school was too late to provide remediation. Besides, we needed to accelerate students rather than remediate them. We did away with summer school and used those funds to create ALP, plus other funds that were reallocated from unaligned programs.

Each school had flexibility in arranging their ALP program and most elected to provide the additional academic support primarily on Saturdays. The school district provided transportation for students and paid classroom teachers their salaried hourly rate to work in the program. For most teachers working in the program, this amounted to another half month or full month salary. Principals recruited the teachers from their faculty, with the idea to challenge these teachers to get students up to speed as quickly as possible.

Each year we measured our progress and could see substantial growth. From Figure 2.1 in Chapter 2, you can see that we started with a composite of 81.9 percent of our students proficient in the 1997–98 school year. Figure 2.2 indicates the composite for African American students was in the 50s and Hispanic/Latino students in the 60s. Five years later, we had moved all students to just above 91 percent. African American students were now at 79.8 percent and Hispanic/Latino students were slightly higher. We had elevated the achievement level for the entire school district and narrowed the achievement gap. We did not make our goal of 95 percent but we were proud of our progress. Subsequently, when we established the next goal, Goal 2008, we renewed our commitment to the 95 percent standard.

For us, our single goal brought us more goodwill in the community than anything else we had done. Every parent knew this goal represented his or her interests. Business people understood how this goal would impact economic vitality in the region. Most importantly, school administrators and teachers were proud to have a goal promoting excellence.

Superintendent's Visits to Schools

Business people often talk about the management tool known as walking around to improve productivity. For instance, Ken Blanchard in the *One-Minute Manager* makes the point that when the manager or CEO spends face time with workers, productivity goes up, defects are reduced, workers appreciate the interaction, and the manager is able to learn while listening—able to develop a first-person perspective on operations. This principle is absolutely no different in the education business. When the superintendent visits schools and classrooms, principals and teachers enjoy showcasing the significant work they're doing educationally. They love the interchange of ideas and the opportunity to provide input on what works and what doesn't work, and it gives the superintendent a chance to recognize and inspire teachers. Visitations also give the superintendent first-hand knowledge of what goes on in the field. Which new programs are paying dividends and which ones are failing miserably? How are students reacting to their environment and instructional programs?

The superintendent should visit schools and classrooms without the typical entourage. This affords an opportunity for teachers and principals to talk directly to the superintendent. This approach eliminates filtering and staff interpretations. Superintendents can gain their own first-hand impressions. Nor should the school or classroom be chosen by anyone other than the superintendent. Sometimes, superintendents will want to announce their intentions to visit a school in advance and sometimes they should just show up and see the school, viewing the principal and the teachers to be in their natural context—the school functioning as it always does each day. Obviously, you want to observe teaching and learning activities, but you also want to observe the change of class, how quickly students get to their next class, the role of the teachers and administrators as traffic police, and how long it takes for the teacher to get the class settled and into the lesson for that timeframe. You want to observe students in the cafeteria, media center, gymnasium, and on the playground. While observing student and staff interactions, you begin to realize the school culture.

By the way, visiting schools is not only done during the day; it's also about attending the athletic events, the theatrical productions, Odyssey of the Mind contests, and the like. As superintendent, on Tuesdays and Fridays, I (Bill) would rotate attendance at athletic events. I never attended these sporting events wearing a necktie or suit jacket. Rather, I was often dressed in a sweatshirt, jeans, and cap. Many times I'd sit in the stands incognito to the people around me. Those were the best of times. Sitting in the crowd, I'd hear the salty language, the opinions of the principal, teachers, and even the superintendent. It was amazing the kind of information that I'd pick up just listening. Sometimes peoples' facts would be correct, sometimes not, but I'd just listen. If eventually I was recognized, then I'd acknowledge who I was, realizing that my ability to watch the game in progress would be over. With school district rivals, I would make a practice of spending one-half of the game on each team's side of the court or field. Sometimes, I'd even do this when teams were visiting from another district. Invariably, I'd learn some new things about our district, some of which was quite unflattering.

While we like to emphasize the academic side of our work in public education, there is certainly much more that we strive to do, including helping our children and youth learn to be good sports. Team coaches may have as much, and sometimes even more, impact on the development of a child than the child's teachers. Attending games will help you keep a check on your coaching staff and how they interact with young people. At the sporting events, you just sit there and observe. When the game is over, pay attention to how orderly attendees leave the game and if you feel the parking lot is safe.

In a given month, you might try for two or three school visits per week on average. This may seem demanding, especially in large school districts where there are many demands on the superintendent's time, but what better way is there for the superintendent to stay up to speed on how schools are functioning? There may be a tendency to visit struggling schools more often than those that are doing well, but be careful. This could send an unintended message that you don't trust your subordinates to do their work improving conditions at the school or that you are micro-managing. Another strategy could be to simply base your visits on geography; be sure to rotate to all parts of the school district. If in the east one day, the next visit may be in the west. If something special is happening on campus, then put that school on your list. If a new principal is in a school, maybe that school should be first on your list. And of course, schools with significant problems should definitely make your list. But sometimes, the choice might simply be that the school is the next one ahead of you on the road and you have some time to stop by and say hello.

When you visit, be prepared for the teacher who might tell you that mistakes have been made with her paycheck and she could be right. You're the superintendent; how will you show your support? One of the nicest letters that I've ever received from a teacher came as a result of my helping to get her paycheck corrected. Sometimes you just have to personally get involved and make the system work for your people. Another time when I was visiting the classroom, I found an art teacher working feverishly with her students and was enjoying myself watching the activity. After about fifteen minutes, the teacher asked if she could help me, and I introduced myself as Bill McNeal. When she asked, "Who's Bill McNeal?" and I said that I was the superintendent, her face dropped and she apologized that she didn't recognize me. Later, when I left the room, I overheard her on the intercom to the front office apologizing to the secretary that she didn't recognize the superintendent, and by the time I returned to my office I had an e-mail from her with another apology. From watching her in the classroom, it was obvious how concerned this teacher was with doing her job well and her apologies only reinforced for me her dedication to teaching. Not recognizing the superintendent was no problem; with her focus on her students, this teacher was doing what she needed to be doing!

The superintendent's job, the school principal's job, and the administrator's job are all demanding and stressful. But every so often, we're reminded why we chose to work in education by something the child, the staff member, the parent, or the community says or does. There is no better place to find these reminders, to renew your spirits, than in the schools surrounded by students and staff.

Superintendent's Challenge to Town Leadership

Wake County is a big, heavily populated area—approximately 864 square miles with three quarters of a million people. That makes for a big school system. Included in the county are twelve municipalities, ranging in size from Raleigh (350,000) to Knightdale (5,000). Although the state is supposed to fund public education, in fact, the county ends up contributing about one third of the annual operating budget. Cities and towns, however, do not allocate local taxes or fees to the operations of the school system, yet they all have high expectations of what the school district should do for them. It had better not be any less than other towns are getting.

The superintendent is used to hearing complaints of perceived or actual inequities among the towns:

- "They have a new school that is attracting new housing developments; when are we going to get one?"
- "Their school has a magnet theme; why not ours?"
- "Their school has only 30 percent poor children (free and reduced-price lunch); ours has 49 percent. What are you going to do about that?"

In a countywide school district like ours, the competition among municipalities is endless. We're willing to bet that even in places where a school district may only represent a single municipality, there will be the same manner of competition, between the west and east sides of the district, between one side of the railroad tracks and the other, between the downtown and the uptown. This kind of competition begets both challenges and opportunities.

In Wake County, one example of taking advantage of this competition to realize an opportunity came when Bill and Tom met with the Town of Knightdale to strengthen a school/community partnership for children, saying that the district could direct some new resources to the town's schools if the town would help make education a priority in the community. The school district wanted more participation from citizens in the town to help their children do better academically. We recognized that the town did not have the higher level of per capita income that some other communities in the county had, but we also argued that being less advantaged economically did not mean students in the town could not learn at a high level. We sought the town's help in finding tutors and mentors for the children.

The mayor and town manager took the challenge. "Education First" in Knightdale became the town council's theme for the next two years. The mayor and Tom went out recruiting in the community, speaking to every church group and club that would have them. In time, hundreds of tutors were signed up and put to work in the schools. Doing their part, the school district allocated some additional resources to support the tutoring effort and the students' subsequent progress was dramatic.

In other situations, a school superintendent might have listened to the town's concerns with a sympathetic ear, explained about the shortage of funds, and waited for the complaining to die down. After all, every community had these same concerns, or at least perceived that they did. Instead, in this situation, the school district purposively made a pact with the town to join together and the superintendent was able to reallocate some resources. With the working relations between town and school district being on a positive footing, the superintendent was also able to attract strong principals to the schools. And, he was able to demonstrate the school/town partnership with other municipalities to show how everyone could contribute to make a difference. During the next several years, over 2,000 tutors across the county were recruited by our municipal partners.

Developing Your Allies and Alliances

One of the issues a superintendent must figure out is how to manage all of the groups you meet. Superintendents meet with lots of groups and they take a tremendous amount of time. But, if you devote quality time on your agenda to spend with them, they become advocates who carry the message. It is not accidental that we have business people who came to the table and brought $2.5 million when we created High Five. It is not accidental that when we were dealing with budget issues, we were able to create a superintendent's finance group made of CFOs from businesses.

One of our motives for organizing a superintendent's finance group arose from a significant debate with the county commissioners regarding how much fund balance (reserve) the school district should carry over from year to year. Their idea was that we shouldn't carry over any; if an emergency arose, we could come to the commissioners and ask for the additional funds. The rub is that they would have to agree that it was a funding issue; we could say we need twenty buses to transport children and they could say, "No, you just need to stop bussing children." What we saw as a funding issue now becomes a program issue. Our response to such challenges from the commissioners was to bring in a team of experts to advise us. Just remember, when you bring in experts, you've got to be ready to accept their findings. If you're just going to bring in "Yes" people, it doesn't help.

We brought in CFOs and had breakfast meetings. We simply asked them questions and put the fund balance topic on the table in the presence of the county manager. They did their research and came back with a finding that other school systems had an average fund balance of 8 percent and, while this is low relative to a business, their ultimate recommendation was that we should have a minimum fund balance of 6 percent. We haven't battled over the fund balance with the county commissioners since.

A leader must always be prepared to look outside the organization and bring in the experts. When our writing scores in the district plummeted, we felt that Educational Testing Services may have some useful approaches and we asked them to come to our school district to train us. When we ran into trouble with our transportation scandal, we organized the resources, both within and outside the school district, to investigate the fraud. We brought in a fraud expert to give us advice on how we should handle the investigation. We put together a committee of folks, made up of the Institute of Government, the State Auditor's office, the County Manager's office, and the State Treasury office. We brought them together in a room and asked, "What's our next step?" We took an idea to the school board that we needed to do a comprehensive audit of the entire school district, and brought in a forensic group to look at every department in the school district. The recommendation was made to the board chair that we needed to conduct the forensic audit and the board chair put the recommendation to the committee rather than the superintendent. When you bring in outsiders like these, you need to be willing to take the risk and willing to deal with the outcomes, whatever they may be. As it turned out, all these people are now allies and advocates for the school district.

The first time Tom Oxholm engaged school district leaders, before he was on the school board, he had been sent by a group called the Luddy Commission with the intent to expose us as wasteful with taxpayers' dollars, etc. When school administrators met with Tom, our decision was to give him whatever he wanted. Tom, being Tom, did something unexpected and asked to get the principals together so that he could talk with them regarding what services they could do without. School leaders said, "Fine, not a problem" and he met with the principals and a group of independent CPAs without the superintendent. After meeting with the principals, rather than reductions in program, he came away with a list of additional services that he wanted for the schools. When Tom issued his report, he issued a fair report and subsequently became one of the strongest advocates for the school system, eventually running for the board of education. Whether professional audits by firms such as MGMT or KPMG, or citizen reviews by the Luddy group, ultimately these and other review groups all said we were good stewards of taxpayer dollars and we were operating without sufficient personnel.

No district runs well unless there is also strong parent support. For instance, you want the PTA to be more than an organization that raises money for the band program or bakes cookies for field trips. During our tenure, we emphasized a role for the PTA to train parent volunteers for the children. From the PTA, we wanted to train as many as 1,000 volunteers, turning this organization into true partners with the school district, helping when students arrive at and leave from the school, helping in the cafeteria, helping in the classroom when the teachers need to step out, etc. The PTA became a willing partner, positioning itself as an organization that could help us achieve our 95 percent goal. Now, in 2007, we believe we have one of the strongest PTAs in the nation, contributing to our success as a school district. The last thing you need is for the PTA to become a gripe group, populated with unhappy campers and their meetings becoming complaint sessions about "my" child's school, "my" child's teacher, etc.

With it being a norm to involve others in our school district processes, our district became involved in the Partnership for Educational Success through a conversation between the superintendent and the head of Wake County Human Services. The initial conversation was about sharing data because we knew that we were serving many of the same children and families. If our two agencies collaborated and pooled our resources, we believed the students and families could be more successful. Yes, we would be careful to ensure that student and family confidences were guarded, but the larger goal here was to coordinate services so as to better serve especially needy students and families.

Each organization assigned a staff member to lead the effort and this joint venture became known as the Partnership for Educational Success, which in turn morphed into a committee process that many of our schools established. With both the schools and Human Services working together to discuss a child's needs, we could better coordinate help for that child. Ultimately, we created a position of parent liaison. Initially, parents didn't trust the schools or Human Services, so the individuals we hired in these positions were themselves parents. They were screened and paid, and their job was to connect with their peers. When they knocked on doors, they were let in. Classic example: The school board policy says that if a child comes to school without immunizations for a period of thirty days, they will be suspended from school. If you're a parent without transportation and may not know where the health department is, how are you going to get your child the immunizations? Now that we were collaborating with Human Services, we brought the nurse to school and gave children their shots. One of the mothers we kept trying to make connections with and get her to come to school continued to refuse. When the parent liaison visited, we learned that the mother wouldn't come to school because her dental work was so bad, she was embarrassed. We were able to help this mother find a dentist who did pro bono work for her. With examples like these, it wasn't long before the chair of the board of directors for Human Services became an advocate for the school system.

Another opportunity to align school allies occurs on Sunday mornings in church. As superintendent, I made a practice of rotating among the churches in our community and was often asked to speak to the congregations. For me, this was an especially enjoyable time, maybe because when you're in the pulpit on Sunday morning, you don't get challenged—there's something about speaking from the pulpit that provides you a different form of authority. It's a very powerful time when, for instance, I would speak about the 27th chapter of Matthew, which emphasizes building your house on a rock—with a solid foundation. Of course, education was a large part of the rock that I would emphasize. Charles Shulz writes a book about Linus building a great castle on the beach that washes away. Linus says, "There's a lesson in this but I don't know what it is." The lesson is about building your house on a rock, not sand.

The Faith Community Steps Up

Businesses establish partnerships with other businesses when the partnership will benefit both parties. You need "X" and I've got "X": I need "Y" and you've got "Y." If our businesses work together, we can both get what we need, strengthen our operations, and have a greater impact. While this same principle is applicable to public education, we tend to be suspicious of entangling alliances. Because we are in the business of "public" education, it could be perceived to be unfair to some parties if we develop exclusive relationships with other parties. Furthermore, when the prospective partner is a church, there is an additional concern with the separation of church and state that we must respect in public education. When our school district set its sights on partnering with the churches in our community, we set out to be inclusive rather than exclusive and we had no intentions of mingling the secular with the sacred. We knew there were common grounds between our needs and those of the faith community upon which we could build a strong partnership that would serve everyone's interests.

There are numerous churches, temples, synagogues, mosques, and other places of worship in our community and these have a significant amount of human, financial, and physical resources. The faith community offers volunteers, it can raise funds, and it has space for programs. Why wouldn't a school district or school principal see these resources as an opportunity to augment the resources of the school and district? Once we began to seriously entertain the notion, we realized that partnering with our faith community was a no-brainer. We only needed to determine what we would ask of the faith community that would also serve their interests.

We knew we could be successful with our appeal to the faith community so long as we created opportunities to partner with us in ways that emphasized social services but that were not controversial. Helping us to raise student achievement met both of these requirements.

When we approached the faith community with the idea of partnering to help us achieve Goal 2003, we were met with more positive interest than we had dared to hope for. Along with organizing tutorial programs, we also asked the faith community to provide computer labs for students and, to our surprise, they stepped up. Finally, we asked that the tutoring programs be provided at no charge and open to any child regardless of his or her race, gender, or faith. In exchange for meeting these terms, we indicated that we would provide school staff to train the volunteers who would work in the programs. By training the volunteers, we were making sure that the tutoring activities would be grade appropriate for children and aligned with our state's standard course of study. Additionally, we indicated that we were also available to speak with church congregations on any issue of concern to the families of the church.

It was very gratifying to see the tremendous response we got from the faith community. At one point, there were about eighty faith facilities conducting tutoring programs and at least twenty had computer labs. The program quickly grew to the point where we could justify hiring a community liaison person with the sole purpose to help set up and monitor these programs in the faith community. This individual sent flyers to the faith leaders urging them to participate. The superintendent committed his energy to supporting the program and frequently attended faith meetings to answer questions and concerns, not all of which were associated with the tutoring program.

The best opportunity for the superintendent to address the faith community was Sunday mornings, rotating among congregations and speaking about education and other needs in the school district. Without crossing the separation between church and state, the superintendent could also make the point that children who attend worship regularly with their parents are likely to have better attendance in school and better grades. Joining the superintendent, there's nothing like having the pastor, priest, or rabbi tell the congregation to get their children to school on time. While in front of these congregations, the superintendent could challenge them to do more, to help with parents who were intimidated by the school setting, to become an outlet to disseminate information about the schools, and to become a voice in support of children's education. This message would resonate even at those faith settings that operated their own schools.

It became routine for the superintendent to be invited to speak before congregations, which led to sending teams of administrators and teachers into the community to respond to parent questions. In one location we would deal with questions about suspension and in another location exceptional children's programs and parent rights. As you might expect, the issue of prayer in the schools would be questioned and we would note that students can pray any time they please. Prayer in the schools doesn't have to mean holding a worship service or demonstrating around the flagpole; students are free to whisper a personal prayer at any time. For an example, we would note that no court in the land has yet ruled that the student who makes a touchdown at Friday night's football game can't give thanks to his faith upon crossing the goal line.

On one memorable occasion, we even addressed an issue of homosexuality when two students in the audience indicated they were lesbians and were subject to being bullied at school. In another situation, a Jewish child wanted to wear a cap other than the yarmulke. The child felt he would be teased and wanted to substitute a baseball cap; however, the school policy was that young men aren't allow to wear caps (other than the yarmulke). Having built relations to the faith community, we were comfortable with reaching out to the Jewish federation for help resolving the issue. Church leaders functioned as mediators to help us to understand the full extent of the issue and came up with a compromise head covering that both the child and the school could accept.

Gaining this kind of access to our faith community had many benefits in addition to the tutoring that our students were receiving—benefits that both partners appreciated. The faith community got to know their families in ways that were different from the traditional relationship forged between church and family. Given that many families participating in the tutoring program were impoverished, the congregations would often go the extra distance to provide coats, book bags, or lunch money, along with social services such as counseling—all because they got to know the families in a different way. Probably the most significant benefit both the school district and the faith community have realized is in the nature of our relationship; we're not at odds with each other and we know that we can work through the common problems and challenges we face.

It's unfortunate when school districts and the faith community get caught up in the separation of church and state. As we've shown, it's possible for these two great institutions to form a partnership that benefits both parties. The school district was able to leverage resources in the faith community to support our need to raise student achievement; the faith community was able to leverage resources in the school district to create a valued service for the community; and the two parties have been able to strengthen bonds of communication and understanding. We were able to raise student achievement, in no small part due to the help that we received from the faith community.

WHAT YOU CAN DO TO IMPROVE

- Continually expand your network and alliances in the community, recognizing that it is everyone's responsibility to educate the community's children
- Create meaningful ways for community members to get involved in the public schools
- Engage the faith community in a meaningful partnership that serves the interests of all

Bringing It All Home

I'm here in Oz, Auntie Em. I'm locked up in the Witch's castle, and I'm trying to get home to you, Auntie Em!

—Dorothy in *The Wizard of Oz*

Home is a place where you are loved unconditionally, a feeling that one is nurtured and cared for by those who are in charge. In Oz, it was Dorothy who was in search of Home. She wanted to return to the security of Auntie Em and Uncle Henry—a safe place. In the educational business, we know that the most successful school districts, schools, and teachers all have the ability to help students feel cared for, secure, and special. The educator who creates an atmosphere of mutual respect and love has a much greater chance of reaching students academically and socially. The real issue here is making sure all students have a support system at school that they can lean on, especially when life becomes a little rocky.

Each of us can tell the story of a favorite teacher, administrator, or school. What made that individual or that school your favorite? We submit that it was how the adults at the school treated you as a person and their desire to see you excel in school and in life. This doesn't mean that they allowed their students to get away with mischievous deeds; to the contrary, they expected more and challenged their students to strive for excellence. The caring spirit they exhibited manifested itself in their willingness to remain after school to give extra help, create programs to augment student performance, and counsel students about school and life.

Too many of our students who are failing, or on the fringe, are there because they are missing the asset of Home—both at home and school. They don't have someone they respect consistently telling them they can do it. They are not being counseled, listened to, having their school work checked, and, yes, chastised when they are wrong as a routine part of their environment. Too often students arrive at school without the asset of Home and have difficulty withstanding the pressures of bullying, testing, physical and emotional developmental issues, peers, gangs, and the many other issues that impact child development.

As well as the home, Home can be found in school, church, and neighborhoods if the environment is child-centered, strives to look long-range, and insists on what is in the best interest of the child. Show us a place where students feel safe and nurtured and we will show you success, not somewhere over the rainbow but right in "Kansas." When we create such an environment, then we understand when our students return years later and remind us that "There is no place like home."

MAKING A HOME OF THE SCHOOL

What is the appeal of Home and can we create some of this atmosphere in our schools?

In the earlier sections of this book, we have discussed Courage, Brains, and Heart, and we view these as three basic values that highly competent leaders will possess and exhibit—wear on their sleeve, so to speak. These three values all bring something different. When we try to summarize what we mean by each of these values, we think of courage, integrity, will, and accountability in the same vein. For us, being willing to take a risk, willing to take the right position even if it is unpopular, and willing to be accountable epitomizes Courage. We think of Brains, questioning, and learning in the same vein. Brains is never being satisfied with what you know, questing to know more, and the desire to continually improve. And, we think of Heart, empathy, and compassion in the same vein. Heart is possessing the feeling that every individual matters, having the ability to stand in their shoes, and the compassion to make a positive difference for each person.

Educational leaders who incorporate these three values in their belief system will be successful and the school is the setting where these leaders should demonstrate such values. Demonstrating these values with students, staff, parents, business leaders, elected officials, and the community will serve you well and help establish the Home for every child that we believe school should be.

Obviously, school is not the child's home; however, we believe there are characteristics of the home that we should emulate in our schools. In the following examples, we develop a number of parallels between home and school that we feel apply equally in both environments.

Unconditional Love

In the home, children experience unconditional love. When faced with the hard knocks of life and those tough periods when it is difficult to see solutions, where does the child turn but to the parents. In school, when children face issues of comparable magnitude (e.g., too much homework, looming tests, being bullied, feeling unaccepted), where can the child turn but to a staff member? In good schools, students will turn to the highly principled adults they find at their school, both teachers and administrators. Will these staff respond with the equivalent of unconditional love? In schools that strive to create the home we are speaking of, the staff will demonstrate this love.

Discipline

At home, when the child misbehaves, the child is disciplined. Does the parent love the child any less? No. In fact, while disciplining the child the parent may say, "This hurts me more than it does you" or, if these very words aren't said, they are probably felt. The parent is hurting for the child. We maintain that the quality administrators, teachers, and staff at school will also have these same feelings. When the child misbehaves at school, discipline the child but love the child all the same. We know that children work best at school when there are structures and parameters and we also know that children work best at school when they feel valued. Manage the students' behavior while you love the children.

High Expectations

In the home, the parent has high expectations for every child. Frequently parents remind the children what their last name is and the parents' expectation that the child will uphold the high standards of the family in behavior, attitudes, and learning. In essence, the parent expects the child will demonstrate good character, responsibility, and productivity, and the parent communicates this expectation in many and numerous ways. The parent's expectations reflect the hopes that the parent holds for the child, to grow up strong and healthy, to live a productive life, to carry on the family lineage. These same high expectations need to be held for students. For example, in the school, the child is reminded constantly that he or she is a Tiger, a Panther, a Timber Wolf—all names for school or classroom or grade-level mascots symbolizing that the student belongs to a clan. And that clan prides itself in being better than the other clans in attitude, athletics, and academics. Frequently, you will hear an administrator or staff on that campus say, "You are a student of this school; we don't behave like that. You are a Martin Mustang and I expect you will act like one!" Administrators and staff must hold the highest expectations for every student, believing in their heart that the athletic teams will defeat other school teams, that student test scores will be superior to those of rival schools, and that students will demonstrate better character than students at other schools.

Pride

In the home, representations of children's success and celebrations of accomplishments abound—parents are proud of their children's accomplishments and want the children to see their pride, along with everyone else who visits the home. There are pictures throughout the home showing the child in various poses and with different family members; the refrigerator is a showcase of the child's accomplishments; the bumper sticker on the family car announces the pride the parent has in the child; and annual social events celebrate major developmental milestones (e.g., birthday parties, graduation parties, soccer banquets, etc.). In the school, these same features need to be present. Are there pictures of the students; are the students' good works posted about the school; are there occasional celebrations of individual as well as group accomplishments? When parents visit the school, can every child take their parents to see representations of their success? Admittedly, it may be easier to do some of these things in the earlier grades than in the later grades, but we maintain that the principle applies across all grade levels. Even in high school, students should be proud of their school and should see evidence that their school is proud of them.

Facing Challenges

In the home, some children may present special challenges such as being handicapped, behaviorally troubled, or not as quick to learn to read as other children in the family. Does the parent write this child off and decide to invest most of the family resources in the other children? No, the parent strives to meet each child's needs and will often search out and secure the additional resources in the home and community that can help the child to progress. The parent may arrange tutoring, may find a mentor for the child, may connect with a parent support group, and so forth. In parallel, a school may be challenged through having a higher incidence of impoverished students than do neighboring schools, or a greater incidence of students for whom English is not their first language, or a number of very demanding students. Does the school write these students off to invest their energies and resources in the students that they feel will be successful? If the school is to provide a home for every child, the answer is no. Rather, the school will seek out—in fact, demand—the additional resources they need to help each and every student succeed. And, if the central office administrators are the leaders they need to be, they will listen to these demands and respond in every way possible to support the school's efforts.

Caretaking

Ultimately, the home is where the child is cared for. Put another way, the child has caretakers who look out for the best interests of the child—whether these be parents, grandparents, aunts and uncles, or other guardians. In a school district, each school also needs caretakers that we maintain will be the leadership provided by the superintendent and central services administrators. Leaders in the central office need to look after the best interests of each and every school. In an article entitled "How to Manage Urban School Districts," Childress, Elmore, and Grossman make this same point, stating that

> Achieving excellence on a broad scale requires a districtwide strategy for improving instruction in the classroom and an organization that can implement it. Only the district office can create such a plan, identify and spread best practices, develop leadership capabilities at all levels, build information systems to monitor student improvement, and hold people accountable for results.[1]

Just as a parent provides the child with unconditional love, enforces discipline as necessary, holds high expectations for the child, takes pride in the accomplishments of the child, faces child-rearing challenges head on, and cares for the overall well-being of the child, so too must educational leaders do the same for their schools and students.

We could continue with drawing parallels between the home and the school, but it is not necessary to make our point. We recognize that not all homes are in fact like the idealized environments we have described above—maybe some homes have all of these characteristics, while most homes have most of these characteristics and some homes have few of these characteristics—but the ideal is what we need to continually strive for. Just think of the home where few of these characteristics are evident. Where will the child from that home find the love, nurturance, and security that he or she needs? We submit that the school can be one such place.

For us, the story of *The Wonderful Wizard of Oz* provides a useful metaphor that describes a structure of core values that leaders can build around. The core values of courage, brains, heart, and home are the bedrock around which leaders can define their leadership. Ultimately, we must make our schools a home for every child.

CONCLUSION

Through the ages, there is much about leadership that has been said. Leadership has been studied, researched, dissected, detailed, defined, and described by many authors and authorities. There is a wealth of information on educational leadership in books, monographs, research archives, and on the Internet. We have done our best to describe for you our perspective on leadership. We believe there is much we can learn from the best practices of business, and we believe there are some fundamental values that are critical to educational leadership. With our closing comments, we will try to distill for you the essence of what leadership means to us.

Heart: Accessibility of the Leader

Two schools of thought exist concerning accessibility. Some believe too much accessibility wears you down and drains you of the energy needed to be a good leader. We believe, however, that making time for people sends a signal that they matter, showing you care for them and that you have heart. In the long run, this second approach is actually encouraging—not draining. Employees will go above and beyond the call of duty, without being asked, if they know that they can make a difference. Following this school of thought, an administrator needs to have staff that will also model this position. If you readily permit personal contact, most staff members will not abuse the privilege. For the leader, personal contact means responding to e-mails and returning phone calls the same day; attending functions throughout the district; being able to call as many people as possible by their names; recognizing accomplishments; and more. Sometimes, it's just being willing to listen when it may not be convenient.

Accessibility also means that you're willing to explain the rationale for your action and that you don't pass this issue off to the subordinate. You made the decision, you answer the critics. You care enough to make yourself personally available. Doing so shows your heart.

Courage: Be Open to Two-Way Communication

When you are accessible to people, remember to listen. There's a good reason we have two ears and only one mouth. As you're listening, does a theme come through? Maybe a parent is calling about a child's classroom assignment. Or maybe your subordinates are expressing frustration with getting their work done to their satisfaction. Or maybe a community group feels that its interests are not being respected or represented in the school district. Or maybe the media feels a responsibility to inform the public on a topical issue. In Wake County, as we listened more and more, we noticed these and other underlying themes about which we could organize a coherent and truthful response.

Be open to two-way communication. Let your defenses down, while asking for, expecting, and respecting honest communication. This takes courage.

Brains: Plan, Organize, and Share the Information

Separate the extraneous stuff from the things you can—and should—actually change. Is there a problem? How often are we hearing about it? If different folks are identifying the same theme, a red flag should go up. Your next step is to investigate. Assign someone to follow up and determine if the problem is real, and to what extent. The really hot issues are ones that have been communicated in many ways—to the board, to the media, by phone, word of mouth—throughout the community. Gather all the information and do your planning. Set up the meetings, share the information, do the brainstorming, research the literature, identify some options, run some numbers, figure the costs, anticipate the hurdles, strategize. As your plans develop, bring more and more individuals and groups into the planning. Your planning will pay dividends when you share the information.

Use your brains. Better yet, expect that everyone will use their brains to jointly find the best course of action.

Bring It All Home and Make the Decision

We get a little nervous when leadership styles are broken out into different camps. No one has all and only all of one leadership style. Generally, we believe that we're democratic leaders, but we can turn into an autocrat with the best of them. Our preference is situational leadership styles; when the situation requires toughness, firmness, and an immediate decision, you've got to be prepared to do that; when the situation requires mercy, you've got to be willing to forgive; when the situation requires an apology, you've got to be willing to admit your shortcoming. Most importantly, you must recognize and accept that the buck stops with the leader.

When you make the decision, then you're also in a monitoring state. If the decision turns out to be a poor one, change it. Why would you stay the course when all the information tells you it's not working? When you change it, say pure and simple that you made the decision, that it did not fix the problem, and now based on the information you've received, you're going to make a different decision. No one expects leaders to be infallible. We all stumble at some time. You can admit you stumbled and grow from it. People will respect you for it.

Look back at your childhood and remember your parents. At some point, you realized they weren't always right. Most of the time, we didn't lose respect for them when they made mistakes; actually, we admired them more if they could admit it. The strong parent who acknowledges "No, that didn't work out, let's change that" only heightens the respect in the children's eyes. The same is true of good leaders.

When you make the decisions, think of that home you grew up in and the people all along the way who helped make you who and what you are today. Keep your thoughts of home and these people in mind as you in turn are now the leader.

> *Be accessible. Be open to two-way communication. Organize and share information. Make the decision. You will do all of these things well if you keep your courage, use your brains, listen to your heart, and create a home for all—students, parents, and staff alike.*
>
> —Bill McNeal and Tom Oxholm

NOTE

1. Childress, S., Elmore, R., & Grossman, A. (2006). How to manage urban school districts. *Harvard Business Review*. Retrieved from http://harvardbusiness sonline.hbsp.harvard.edu/b02/en/common/item_detail.jhtml?id=R0611B

It is interesting to note that these authors begin their article by stating, "Big-city school systems aren't businesses and can't be managed like them." However, we find that many of the ideas they describe in the article do in fact have parallels in best business practices.

Afterword

Looking back, now that we're both no longer with the Wake County Public School System, we believe there were a number of factors that contributed to the district's success: (a) a single, focused goal that aligned the curriculum, created a funding structure, and forced high expectations; (b) the expectation that there can be no excuses for any subgroup of students; (c) the effort to maintain diverse student populations in our schools and classrooms, reflecting that of the larger community; (d) the involvement of business in education, with the largest number of business partners of any district in the state, if not the nation; (e) the involvement of the faith community and their willingness to provide tutoring and mentoring across the county free of charge; (f) the involvement of thousands of parent volunteers, with many helping in the area of literacy; (g) a visionary board of education that was totally driven to excellence and understood the bottom line is superior performance for all children; and (h) tremendous administrators and instructional staff that bought into and took ownership of the success for all children.

Looking ahead, we can identify a couple of red flags that may or may not be unique to Wake County: (a) the ceaseless growth in student enrollment, and the ability to fund it and house the children, has become the tail that wags the dog, derailing the district's focus on instructional issues; (b) the local as well as national clamor for neighborhood schools that could result in racial or economic isolation, essentially a resegregation of our children; and (c) a shortage of high quality administrators and teachers, in part due to retirement of baby boomers and in part due to low respect for the field of education.

Short of building a wall around the boundaries of Wake County, we can't do much about slowing or reversing the growth of the school district and we probably shouldn't complain too much about growth, as it does reflect a level of prosperity. However, there are measures that we can take regarding the second and third conditions above. In our school policies, we can continue to emphasize the importance of maintaining diverse student bodies in all of our schools. And, in our administrative practices we can continue to develop and seek out the most courageous, most talented, and most caring leaders to place in charge of our children and youth.

The research is clear that high quality administrators and teachers make the difference in the quality of a child's education. All the other elements that go into a school district are supports without which it would be difficult to operate, but it is the staff that makes the difference. If this is true, and it is, then our nation must respect the profession. The quality of our schools is linked directly to the quality of the administrators and teachers.

In our introductory chapter, we argue that educational leaders must become adept at employing business practices and procedures if we are to successfully educate the children and youth of our nation's public schools. In this book, we have drawn many parallels between business and educational practices. Generally speaking, we believe that there is much that educators can learn from business principles and practices no matter where you reside, the size of your school district, or the budget you have to work with. Business and educational leaders alike must be accomplished with motivating and managing people to turn out a better product. At the end of the day, we believe that the business of education is taking care of your people.

To all school leaders, administrators, and teachers alike, we wish you the best. Yours is a hard task and a noble profession. As you travel the yellow brick road to excellence, keep up your courage, be smart, have heart, and make a home of your school.

Resources

Appendix A

Selected Readings and Resources Organized by Chapter and Section

2. LEADERSHIP AND COURAGE

Accountability

The Center for Public Education. (2006). *A guide to standards-based reform.* Available online at http://www.centerforpubliceducation.org/site/c.kjJXJ5 MPIwE/b.1505663/k.1F96/A guide to standardsbased_reform.htm

Although the particulars vary from state to state, all states but Iowa currently have developed a set of standards that defines education for its students. Standards represent end points in a student's career and, whether at the end of each grade or the end of elementary, middle, or high school, the goal is the same: to make sure schools are providing all students with the education they need to lead meaningful, productive lives in the new century.

Office of Curriculum and School Reform Services. (2006). *The ABCs of public education.* Raleigh, NC. Available online at http://www.ncpublicschools .org/docs/accountability/reporting/abc/2005–06/abcsbrochure.pdf

North Carolina's ABCs of Public Education are defined and discussed on this Web site.

Wake County Public School System. (2006). *ABCs results.* Raleigh, NC. Available online at http://www.wcpss.net/test-scores/nc-abcs/

This Web page shows the ABC results by year from 2000 to 2006 for Wake County Public School System.

Author's Note: EDSTAR, Inc. a Raleigh-based firm specializing in educational program evaluations, worked closely with Bill and Tom to develop this annotated bibliography.

Focus on Learning. (1998). Turning around low-performing schools: A guide for state and local leaders. *Raising the stakes: Setting high standards for performance.* Available online at http://209.85.165.104/search?q=cache: MIEV07 xKBuwJ:www.ed.gov/pubs/turning/stakes.html+education+%22Setting+ high+standards%22&hl=en&ct=clnk&cd=5&gl=us

This article describes several school systems that successfully set high standards and how this helped the students become high achievers. (This is an archived article.)

Hess, D., Rogovsky, N., & Dunfee, T. W. (2002). The next wave of corporate community involvement. *California Management Review, 44*(2), 110–125. Available online at http://lgst.wharton.upenn.edu/dunfeet/Documents/ Articles/CMRNext.pdf

This article discusses how businesses and corporations are becoming more and more involved in community affairs, which is advantageous to the community, the corporations, and the students. When corporations become involved in educational affairs, everybody wins.

Gorman, L. (1997, June). *Running schools like a business?* Independence Institute. Available online at http://www.i2i.org/main/article.php?article_id=138

In this opinion editorial, Linda Gorman describes similarities and differences between schools and businesses.

Leadership

Young, P. (2007). The principal as troublemaker. *Education World.* Available online at http://www.education-world.com/a_admin/admin/admin481.shtml

Paul Young is a retired principal and past president of the National Association of Elementary School Principals (NAESP). In this article, he describes how being a troublemaker (with a capital "T") is sometimes necessary. "Principals must be resilient and able to persevere. Those who accept inequality or tolerate injustice will fail. It is incumbent upon every school management team to adopt procedures for solving problems, challenging practices, and altering procedures. . . . If the leaders of the management team won't facilitate or engage in necessary discussions, an ambitious principal or more must shake things up—and 'cause trouble' until they do."

Hord, S. M. (2002). *Blueprints for success.* National Staff Development Council. Available online at http://ali.apple.com/ali_media/Users/1000742/files/ others/BlueprintsforSuccess.pdf

Six states received a large grant from the Bill & Melinda Gates Foundation to provide professional development for their superintendents and principals. The training was to cover leadership, whole systems change, and technology integration. North Carolina participated. This text provides a study of the most promising practices employed by the different states that participated.

Hopkins, G. (2005). Principals identify top ten leadership traits. *Education World.* Available online at http://www.education-world.com/a_admin/admin/admin190.shtml

Education World surveyed forty-three successful principals and asked them to list the top ten traits they believe a school leader should have. Having a clear vision, being visible, being trustworthy, and including others in decision making topped the lists.

Daniels, H., Bizar, M., & Zemelman, S. (2000) *Rethinking high school: Best practice in teaching, learning, and leadership.* Portsmouth, NH: Heinemann Publishers.

This book describes how educational leaders can ensure students are challenged to their full potential, while also discussing the importance of community involvement and other attributes that make high schools work.

Air War College. (2006). *Leadership, ethics, and command central.* U. S. Air Force. Available online at http://www.au.af.mil/au/awc/awcgate/awc-ldr.htm

Although the differences between leading a command and running a school system are numerous, leaders of both share many core values. The military has done much research in what makes a good leader, and this site from the U. S. Air Force's Air War College provides many links to other sites that discuss important traits that all good leaders share.

Organizing Your Leadership

Goodwin, D. K. (2005). *Team of rivals: The political genius of Abraham Lincoln.* New York: Simon & Schuster.

Abraham Lincoln selected his three Republican opponents in the presidential race to occupy his cabinet after he was elected. All three, William H. Seward, Salmon P. Chase, and Edward Bates, were nationally known and somewhat humiliated that this backwoods, Illinois rail-splitter had defeated them. All three had disdain for him. Lincoln chose to surround himself with these disgruntled rivals and let them share in the decision processes during one of the United States's most turbulent periods. All three came to respect and admire him. Bill McNeal, like Lincoln, believes that when you invite your opponents to sit at the table, rather than shut them out, you can eliminate much disfavor and disgruntlement. And because your opponents may have ideas you hadn't thought of, they can usually bring something new to the table and eventually become allies.

Clark, J., & Picard, J. (1989). *Laying down the law: Joe Clark's strategy for saving our schools.* Washington, DC: Regnery Publications.

A former Army drill instructor, Joe Clark entered Eastside High in Paterson, New Jersey, and turned the school from a disorderly, drug-infested institution into a model school. Although Clark's leadership methods differ somewhat from Bill McNeal's (Clark expelled 300 students during his first week as principal), he does offer another style of leadership. Clark was named one of the nation's ten "Principals of Leadership" in 1986, and President Reagan offered him a White House post as Policy Advisor, which he turned down.

Farkas, S., Johnson, J., Duffett, A., Foleno, T., & Foley, P. (2001). *Trying to stay ahead of the game: Superintendents and principals talk about school leadership.* New York: Public Agenda. Available online at http://www.wallacefounda tion.org/NR/rdonlyres/0E8B521F-9CD5–4A32ACB2-BAC0B569B2FC/ 0/ahead_of_the_game.pdf

This Public Agenda report, funded by the Wallace Foundation, is based on in-depth surveys of 853 randomly-selected public school super-intendents and 909 randomly-selected public school principals. They discuss the hardships they face and how bureaucracy often ties their hands. Most named insufficient funding as their most pressing issue. Many of the principals were on board with new accountability requirements. All believe that requirements for leadership in schools have transformed education, and leaders must be multitaskers with knowledge in many areas.

McKay, J., & Peterson, M. (2004, February). Recruiting board members: Should superintendents have a role in the process? A survey finds divided views. *School Administrator.* Available online at http://findarticles.com/p/articles/ mi_m0JSD/is_2_61/ai_113417052/pg_1

McKay and Peterson surveyed superintendents in two Midwestern states. Demographically, 61 percent had more than sixteen years of experience as superintendents. The surveys asked the superintendents to respond to a series of scenarios and how they would handle them. The results are provided in this article.

Communicating With Your Public

Geiger, P. E. (2002, April). Education in America: Schools and strategies that work. *School Business Affairs.* Available online at http://asbointl.org/ASBO/files/ ccPageContentDOCFILENAME000826705546ASBO_April_2002.pdf

This article discusses many attributes of a school leader, including the importance of communicating with the public. The author believes that forward-thinking superintendents are often thwarted in their efforts to hire public relations representatives, because many school boards think it would be a waste of money. He believes strong leaders can prevail, however.

George, C., & Keung Hui, T. (2006, September 19). 4 get time in school fraud. *The News and Observer*. Raleigh, NC. Available online at http://www.newsob server.com/211/story/488122.html

Although the articles that ran locally were numerous, this one was printed near the end of the fraud ordeal that could have embarrassed Wake County, had Bill McNeal tried to cover it up. Instead, he welcomed the media with open arms and kept the public informed of the ongoing investigation. This link provides the full story in sidebars, as well as links to other *News and Observer* articles covering the scandal.

Summerford Accountancy, PC, Fraud and Forensic Accountants. (2006). *Fraud vulnerability assessment prepared for the Wake County Board of Education.* Birmingham, AL. Available online at http://www.wcpss.net/audit/summer ford.pdf

After the scandal of fraudulent purchase orders within the Wake County Public School System, Summerford Accountancy was hired to perform a fraud vulnerability assessment. They identified no further fraud but did find several areas in which fraud could take place and go unnoticed for a period of time. They made several recommendations to avoid this, and their entire report is available online at the Wake County Public School System Web site.

Kearns, H. (1995, November). Have you thanked your reporter lately? *School Administrator*. Available online at http://findarticles.com/p/articles/mi_m0JSD/ is_10_52/ai_77196864

Kearns discusses how educators can use the media effectively to champion their causes and announce their successes. The relationship between the media and educators need not be hostile; both can benefit from an open relationship.

Molyneux, N. (n.d.). Building effective websites—defining my website. *Dotography*. Available online at http://www.dotography.com/assets/media/dotography-defining-my-website-v2.7.pdf

This article is an excellent how-to on building effective school Web sites. It contains an outline of major links, with minor links that can fall under each one.

Swann, P. A. (2006, May). Got web? Investing in a district website: An effective site can help you reach your organizational goals. *School Administrator*. Available online at http://findarticles.com/p/articles/mi_m0JSD/is_5_63/ ai_n16418919

Most schools have moved far enough into the information age to have set up a Web site. But many Web sites are a mish-mash of unrelated information, much of it entertaining but useless. Other Web sites take the opposite approach—information overload with no order. In this article, Swann discusses what makes a good Web site and tells you what to avoid.

Local.com Corporation. (2008). *Search for local businesses, products, and services*. Available online at http://www.local.com

The home page of this Web site will ask what you're looking for and where. You can put "local cable stations" and your city and state (and address, if desired) in these boxes, then click on "Search." It will list all the local stations, with their addresses and phone numbers, and how far they are (in miles) from you.

3. LEADERSHIP AND BRAINS

Goal Setting and Planning

Wake County Public School System. (2006). *Goal and mission*. Available online at http://www.wcpss.net/goal-mission.html

The entire Goal 2008 is laid out on the Wake County Public School System's Web site.

Nutt. P. (2000, October). Effective school boards produce strong schools. *Multimedia Schools*. Available online at http://www.infotoday.com/MMSchools/oct00/nutt.htm

A school board's measure of success goes beyond student achievement, parental participation, and community involvement, although these do measure success. Nutt discusses how strong school boards can affect the success of an entire school system.

Wake County Public School System. (2002). *News from WCPSS' Continuous Improvement Conference: McNeal reveals vision for 2002–2003*. Raleigh, NC. Available online at http://www.wcpss.net/news/2002_july_conf/updates.html

At this Wake County Public School System Web site, highlights from Bill McNeal's Continuous Improvement Conference are discussed. Pictures of key players are also available here.

Nadler, D. (2004, May). Building better boards. *Harvard Business Review.* Available online at http://harvardbusinessonline.hbsp.harvard.edu/hbsp/hbr/articles/article.jsp?ml_action=get-article&articleID=R0405G&ml_page=1&ml_subscriber=true

In this executive summary, David Nadler discusses what boards must do if they are dissatisfied with "lowest common denominator" results. Boards must set clear goals and agendas and work toward them.

Frisch, B., & Chandler, L. (2006, June). Off-sites that work. *Harvard Business Review.* Available online at http://harvardbusinessonline.hbsp.harvard.edu/b01/en/common/item_detail.jhtml?id=R0606H

Frisch and Chandler discuss what makes for good off-site planning and strategy meetings. They maintain that if you and your board members spend several days a year rafting down a river together, you'll become very good at rafting down rivers. But, if you spend time on essential conversations and planning, you can transform your "business." Although the article is business oriented, they discuss strategies that would work for the "business" of education, as well.

Training Leaders

De León, A. G. (2006, Fall). The school leadership crisis: Have school principals been left behind? *The Carnegie Reporter, 4* (1). Available online at http://www.carnegie.org/reporter/13/crisis/index3.html

De León discusses how the typical path to becoming a school leader has changed in the past ten years. In the past, aspiring principals were usually a former athlete or coach, almost exclusively male, who would earn an MBA at night school to obtain certification. She discusses how no reasonable, successful company would choose a CEO this way. But, as accountability has become more important, the role of principals has become extremely complex. The preparation of principals has become increasingly important.

Iacocca, L. (2007). *Where have all the leaders gone?* New York: Simon & Schuster.

Lee Iacocca is a self-made leader who is known for saving the Chrysler Corporation from financial ruin. He also oversaw the renovation of Ellis Island and currently oversees the Iacocca Institute for Leadership. He has rubbed elbows with many world leaders, including nine presidents, heads of states, and many CEOs of large companies. At eighty-two years old, he has much to say about leadership.

Measuring Success

U. S. Department of Education. (2004). *A guide to education and No Child Left Behind.* Available online at http://www.ed.gov/nclb/overview/intro/guide/index.html

The Department of Education provides this online guide to No Child Left Behind. Much more information about this policy can be found at their Web site.

North Carolina Department of Public Instruction. (2007). *NCLB and ABCs changes for North Carolina.* Available online at http://www.ncpublicschools.org/docs/nclb/abcayp/overview/abcaypchanges.pdf

This article provides information about how North Carolina has changed policies as NCLB and ABC have transformed education.

Herman, J., & Winters, L. (1992). *Tracking your school's success: A guide to sensible evaluation.* Los Angeles, CA: Los Angeles Center for Research on Evaluation, Standards, and Student Testing, University of California.

This book discusses how to evaluate and monitor a school's academic progress and how to address its shortcomings. Evaluations can then be used to determine what changes can be made to improve achievement. The book covers a six-step decision-making process that suggests ways to (1) identify and report successes; (2) manage instrument and data collection; (3) score and summarize data; (4) analyze and interpret information; (5) act on findings; and (6) continue program monitoring.

Beyer, B. (1995). *How to conduct a formative evaluation.* Alexandria, VA: Association for Supervision and Curriculum Development.

With accountability becoming more important, anecdotal evidence is no longer justification for continuing programs. This book is a how-to manual on conducting formative evaluations for educational programs. Formative evaluations are meant to be performed as a program is being implemented to determine what is working and what is not, based on research.

Dollars and Sense

Arif, M., Kulonda, D. J., & Smiley, F. M. (2005). Business and education as push-pull processes: An alliance of philosophy and practice. *Education, 125.* Available online at http://www.questia.com/PM.qst?a=o&d=5009846923

The authors quote Weidmer and Harris when discussing how schools have become much more businesslike in the past decade: "Customers are the students, parents and the community, and quality schools of the 21st century must begin the process by understanding the needs of this customer base."

Wake County Public School System. (2001). *The school connection.* Available online at http://www.wcpss.net/online_newsletters/the_school_connec tion/newsletters/2001/4_6_2001-tsconnection.html

This is a general discussion of the 2001–02 budget, and how it was needed to meet Goals 2003.

Wake County Public School System. (2001). *Board of education's 2001–02 budget request.* Available online at http://www.wcpss.net/budget/2001–02-budget-request/index.html

Budgets of the Wake County Public School System for the last eight years and the request for 2008–09 are also available here. Be sure to read the opening twenty pages with references to key sections of the budget document.

4. LEADERSHIP AND HEART

Students Matter Most

The Education Trust. (2006). *Yes we can: Telling truths and dispelling myths about race and education in America.* Washington, DC. Available online at http://www2.edtrust.org/NR/rdonlyres/DD58DD01–23A4–4B89–9FD8-C11BB072331E/0/YesWeCan.pdf

This report soundly rejects the myth that low academic achievement is inevitable among children of color and students from low-income families, and provides examples of high-minority and high-poverty schools where children perform at high levels.

Fletcher, A. (2005) *Meaningful student involvement guide to students as partners in school change.* Seattle, WA: HumanLinks Foundation. Available online at http://www.soundout.org/ladder.html

In this article, Fletcher discusses allowing students to be involved in decision-making processes beyond choosing the theme for the prom or the school fight song. He believes students can be involved in everything from deciding what courses should be taught to filling staff vacancies.

Osberg, J., & Pope, D. (2006). Students matter in school reform: Leaving fingerprints and becoming leaders. *International Journal of Leadership in Education,* 9(4), 329–343.

The authors studied three schools that involved students in their reform efforts. Students were allowed to give input about problems, and design and help implement the reform. The experience was beneficial for everyone. Not only did the students feel as if they were part of the system, but they gained insight and leadership characteristics.

Live Wire Media. (2008). *Character education: Free resources, materials, lesson plans.* Available online at http://www.goodcharacter.com/

This is an excellent source for student character education.

Teachers Matter Most

Peterson, P. E. (2006). Of teacher shortages and quality: Now that we can identify good teachers, let's reward them. *Education Next*, Spring, 2006. Available online at http://findarticles.com/p/articles/mi_m0MJG/is_2_6/ai_n16118686

Peterson argues that a man may carry a valid driver's license, but that's no guarantee he'll stay in his lane. Likewise, teachers may have all the right certification, but it doesn't necessarily make them good teachers. The current focus on credentials has overshadowed the problem of genuinely good teachers—those who inspire students despite overwhelming odds.

Ferriter, W. (2005). Principals matter. *A teacher's journal 13.* Available online at http://www.wcpss.net/announcements/archives/2005/08/a_teachers_jour_8.html

The Wake County Public School System Web site allows teachers to post short articles on topics of their choice under their link "A Teacher's Journal." Many take advantage of it, and a variety of subjects are discussed. In this following "journal entry," a Wake County teacher discusses the attributes of a good principal.

Wake County Public School System. (2002). *Teacher advisory council works to help Wake teachers and students.* Available online at http://www.wcpss.net/news/poston/teacher_council/

This article discusses Bill McNeal's Teacher Advisory Council, including its inception, its makeup, and the good it does for the school system.

Parents Matter Most

Rutherford, B., & Billig, S. H. (1995). Eight lessons of parent, family, and community involvement in the middle grades. *Phi Delta Kappan, 77.* Available online at http://www.questia.com/PM.qst?a=o&se=gglsc&d=5000352133

In an excerpt of their study on parent and community involvement in education, the authors examined school/family partnerships in the middle grades (Grades 6–8). Research on the potential effects of family involvement in early childhood education and in the elementary grades presents a favorable picture. Their research focused on three areas: comprehensive districtwide programs, school restructuring, and adult/child learning programs.

Kakli, Z., Kreider, H., Little, P., Buck, T., & Coffee, M. (2006). *Focus on families! How to build and support family-centered practices in after school.* Boston: Harvard Family Research Project. Available online at http://gseweb.harvard.edu/hfrp/content/projects/afterschool/resources/families/guide.pdf

In this article, the authors discuss why engaging families in education is important and effective methods that help to engage families. They also profile several school districts that made concerted efforts to build family-centered practices.

Harris, E., & Wimer, C. (2004). *Engaging families with out-of-school time learning.* Boston: Harvard Family Research Project. Available online at http://gseweb.harvard.edu/hfrp/content/projects/afterschool/resources/snapshot4.html

Harris and Wimer discuss out-of-school time (OST) programs that engage families in students' education. They evaluate different OST programs to determine which are most effective and also what schools can do to engage families.

Johnson, J. L., Niedrich, K., & Lewis, R. G. (2003). *Removing obstacles to parent involvement 2002–2003.* Raleigh, NC: EDSTAR, Inc. Available online at http://www.edstar.biz/edstar/reports/file/Family_Involvement.pdf

Parent work schedules are the primary barrier that prevent parents from participating in school activities with their children. In this report, the authors discuss the importance of involving parents in their children's education and ways to deal with the many obstacles parents face that hinder this.

National Center for Education Statistics. (2005a). Percentage of elementary and secondary school children whose parents were involved in school activities, by selected child, parent, and school characteristics: 1999 and 2003. *Digest of Education Statistics 2005: Table 23.* Washington, DC: U.S. Department of Education. Available online at http://nces.ed.gov/programs/digest/d05/tables/dt05_023.asp?referer=list

Data now show that regardless of race or annual income, parents spend time with their children and the poor or minority children are not being deprived of cultural activities or quality attention. The National Center for Educational Statistics recently did a study on parents' interaction with children and found that although white parents are slightly more likely than African American parents to take their children to a play or concert, African American parents are more likely to take their children to a library, zoo, art gallery, or museum. And although Hispanic parents are much less likely than African American or white parents to take their children to a play, concert, or other live show, they are only slightly less likely to visit a library or museum than whites, and far more likely than African Americans or whites to visit a zoo or aquarium.

National Center for Education Statistics. (2005b). Percentage of kindergartners through fifth-graders whose parents were involved in education-related activities, by selected child, parent, and school characteristics: 1999 and 2003. *Digest of Education Statistics 2005: Table 24*. Washington, DC: U.S. Department of Education. Available online at http://nces.ed.gov/programs/digest/d05/tables/dt05_024.asp?referer=list

This table shows that, contrary to popular myths, almost no difference exists between families with incomes over $30,000 and poorer families spending time telling stories to their children or doing arts and crafts. According to the National Center for Education Statistics 2005 Digest of Educational Statistics, the wealthier the parents, the *less* time they spend helping their children with homework: An average of 15 percent of parents who earn less than $20,000 per year help their children with homework five or more days per week, compared with only 11 percent of parents who earn more than $35,000 per year. Only 9.5 percent of parents who earned more than $75,000 helped their children with homework five or more times per week. Similar disparities were true for three and four days per week.

Involving the Entire Village

National Parent Teachers Association. (2007). *National standards for parent/family involvement programs.* Available online at http://www.pta.org/archive_article_details_1118251710359.html

The National PTA Web site includes links to many articles on how to effectively engage parents and activities PTAs can do to improve the quality of schools. This article discusses six characteristics of programs found to effectively get parents involved in school activities.

North Carolina's Communities in Schools. (n.d.). *What is Communities in Schools (CIS)?* Available online at http://www.cisnc.org/code/wwhw.htm

Although twenty-seven states have Communities In Schools (CIS) programs, at North Carolina's CIS Web site, they succinctly discuss what the organization does, how it works in North Carolina, and how it benefits everyone. National CIS information is available at http://www.cisnet.org/default.asp

Harlow, K., & Baenen, N. (2004). Partnerships for educational success 2002–2003: Implementation and outcomes. *Eye on Evaluation*, May 2004. Raleigh, NC: Wake County Public School System Evaluation and Research Department. Available online at http://www.wcpss.net/evaluation-research/reports/2004/0409partnership_edu.pdf

This evaluation discusses the goals of Wake County's Partnerships for Educational Success and how it set about to achieve them.

Brown, L. J. (2001, May). Networking with the community. *School Business Affairs, 67*(5): 23–26.

In this article, Brown discusses the importance of involving the entire community in education affairs. She also discusses effective strategies to get the community on board with educational goals.

Resnick, M. (2000). *Communities count: A school board guide to public engagement.* Alexandria, VA: National School Boards Association.

This book, published by the National School Boards Association, is written for school board members and is a basic how-to manual on engaging the community with public education.

U.S. Department of Education. (1999, September). *Faith communities joining with local communities to support children's learning. Good ideas.* Available online at http://www.ed.gov/pubs/goodideas/examples.html

This article provides eight examples of faith communities who set up programs to help local school children achieve.

Appendix B

Criteria for a Superintendent's Evaluation

The following ten criteria were set by the Wake County Board of Education for Bill McNeal's 2004–05 evaluation. These criteria exemplify the school board's annual performance evaluation of the superintendent. Targets were set for each criterion and we have provided examples of these targets; some of the criteria had multiple targets.

1. Goal 2008: Lead to improved academic performance in reading, math, and high school courses.

   Target: +1 percent from '04 on the End-of-Grade Composite (reading and math) for Grades 3–5.

2. Goal 2008: Increase student achievement measured by growth (a metric in the state's ABCs plan for student achievement).

   Target: Increase the number of NCLB subgroups meeting high growth.

3. Goal 2008: Evaluate programs identified by the board for effectiveness, efficiency, and/or alignment with Goal 2008.

   Target: Assess character education program for effectiveness and implementation; develop character education policy for board consideration.

4. Staffing: Improve recruitment and reduce turnover to ensure quality staffing.

   Target: The turnover of probationary teachers will be less than 15 percent.

5. Annual Satisfaction Surveys: Improve satisfaction with school safety and student achievement as evidenced on annual surveys of staff, parents, and students.

   Target: 90 percent "Good" or "Excellent."

6. Budget and Financing: Superintendent's Budget Request.
   a. Prepare FY 05 budget focused on Goal 2008, highlighting alignment with Goal and identifying necessary resources.
   b. Analyze for alignment with revenue, growth, and inflation projections.
   c. Provide documentation on specific programs aligned with Goal 2008.
   d. Provide County information on differences between their planning model and WCPSS planning and program needs.

   Target: Multi-year projections; supporting business cases for additional funding; input from new group of finance advisors; improved understanding of fiscal needs of individual departments; timely reports of process to the board.

7. System Leadership: Improve internal/external communications to achieve public appreciation of system strengths and values through comprehensive plan to achieve strategic goals.

   Target: Show evidence of effort through initiatives.

8. System Leadership: Continue to improve student assignment process including better long-range planning for healthy schools through continued implementation of community engagement model.

   Target: Improved board and community satisfaction.

9. System Leadership: Continue efforts to ensure that all school models are attractive and healthy, through demonstrating multi-year planning to the board.

   Target: Report to the board.

10. Personal Leadership: Superintendent's personal efforts to achieve goals by leading personnel and building community confidence, through communication of system goals, values and achievements, personal work ethic, community involvement, senior staff development, and innovation.

    Target: Board satisfaction and succession plans in place.

Appendix C

Recommendation for National
Superintendent of the Year

When Bill McNeal was being considered by the American School Administrators Association, then North Carolina Governor Jim Hunt wrote a letter of recommendation for Bill. With Governor Hunt's permission, we have included the complete letter here as a testimony to the nature of Bill's leadership, the leadership of the Wake County Board of Education, and the accomplishments of the school district. Written September 25, 2003, then Governor Hunt had the following to say:

North Carolina Association of School Administrators
214 New Bern Place
Raleigh, NC 27601

To Whom It May Concern:

I write this letter to whole-heartedly endorse the nomination of Superintendent William (Bill) R. McNeal, Jr. of the Wake County Public School System in Raleigh, North Carolina, as a candidate for the 2004 National Superintendent of the Year.

Bill McNeal exemplifies courageous and innovative leadership. For example, in his urban school district that now has 109,000 students in 127 schools, he challenged the School Board in 1998 to set the audacious goal of having 95% of students in grades 3–8 scoring at grade level or above in five years. (The scores then were about 82%.) While the goal was not quite attained, the scores reached in 2003 were an amazing 90.4% in reading and 92.3% in math. SAT scores of 1067 are the highest of the state's urban districts and exceed the national average by 41 points. Dropout rates (grades 7–12) have declined to the lowest level ever of 2.3%.

The average teacher turnover rate has been less than 10% for the past three years.

As Chairman of the National Commission on Teaching and America's Future, I am always looking out for best superintendent leadership in improving teaching. Bill McNeal is a national model. He created the first Wake Task Force on Teacher Excellence in cooperation with Wake Education Partnership. Through this initiative, he assembled a distinguished group of teachers, professors, executives and parents to review national research about schools that foster excellence among classroom teachers. From this he launched a comprehensive plan to engage and motivate teachers in Wake County including the Teacher Advisory Committee, a workgroup to create a new career pathway for teachers, a training program for future leaders among teachers and a sustained commitment by business to address needs associated with teacher professionalism.

But there are two special accomplishments of the Wake County system that I would urge the Committee to consider. First, the system under Bill McNeal's strong moral leadership has insisted on real diversity in its schools. This has antagonized some people who demand strict "neighborhood schools" for their children—regardless of the effect on schools and students in other areas. But this diversity has resulted in school student bodies in which all students are more likely to learn, regardless of race, religion or family income. The second accomplishment is that of student learning in this diverse district: 98% of Wake County's schools either met or exceeded learning goals this past year. A total of 124 of the 127 schools met their goals of at least a full year's growth or more.

Bill McNeal is a familiar face in the community. With over 200 community appearances annually including TV, radio, and newspaper interviews; elected officials' meetings; town meetings; civic club and church presentations; local club and school-sponsored organization events, he is accessible to the community. His passion for sharing the story and vision of the Wake County Public School System is relentless. His energy for engaging all facets of the community is constant. He carries the banner for public education for all the public's children proudly and with steadfast commitment. In his three years as superintendent, he has visited every school in his district, some more than once, and has participated in school-sponsored activities and events too numerous to recount.

The Wake County Public School System has recently received some wonderful national attention for its academic success, for its strong system of schools, and for its diversity philosophy in a time when neighborhood schools are resurfacing. It has been named as one of the 100 best school systems in the nation by *Money* magazine. Washington Elementary

School was named the best magnet school in the nation. And, it was recently feature on NBC Nightly News.

I have never known a better superintendent in America and I strongly recommend him for your 2004 National Superintendent of the Year.

Sincerely,

James B. Hunt, Jr.
Governor of North Carolina

Appendix D

National Recognitions for WCPSS and Wake County

Over the years, Wake County and the Wake County Public School System have received numerous accolades for the quality and excellence of its community. The Raleigh Chamber of Commerce has collected many of these recognitions and posted them on the Internet. Below, we've selected a few of these accolades that feature business and education in the county. (For more information on these and many other recognitions of the county and school district, visit www.raleigh-wake.org/index.cfm?fuseaction=page&filename=accolades.html.)

2007

Top 10 Metro Areas for Job Growth
—*Business 2.0*, May 2007

#1 Best Place for Business and Careers (Raleigh, NC)
—*Forbes*, April 2007

#1 Best US City for Jobs (Raleigh-Cary, NC)
—Forbes.com, February 2007

#1 School District in the Nation for Certified Teachers (Wake County)
—National Board of Certified Teachers, January 2007
Gold Rating (Wake County Schools)
—*Expansion Management's Education Quotient, January 2007*

2006

#1 Area for Tech Business (Raleigh-Durham, NC)
—Silicon Valley Leadership Group, September 2006

#2 Best Place for Business & Careers (Raleigh, NC)
—*Forbes*, May 2006

#3 Most Educated City (Raleigh, NC)
—*American Community Survey*, US Census Bureau, 2004 (Released January 2006)

2005

Top 20 Business Opportunity Metro (Raleigh-Cary, NC)
—*Expansion Management*, July 2005

#5 Knowledgeable Workforce (Raleigh-Cary, NC)
—*Expansion Management*, July 2005

#2 Most Educated City (Raleigh, NC)
—*US Census Bureau-American Community Survey*, 2003 Survey (Released April 2005)

#2 Best Public Education System (Raleigh-Cary, NC)
—*Expansion Management*, April 2005

2004

#2 Best Place for Business (Raleigh-Durham, NC)
—*Forbes*, May 2004

#6 Best Public School System (Raleigh-Durham-Chapel Hill MSA)
—*Expansion Management's MSA Education Quotient Rankings*, April 2004

2004 National Superintendent of the Year (Bill McNeal, Wake County Public Schools)
—*American Association of School Administrators*, 2004

#3 Best Education in the Biggest Cities (Wake County Schools)
—*Forbes*, February 2004

2003

#1 Best Place to Live
—*MSN House & Home*, July 2003

#1 Best Place to Live and Work
—*Employment Review*, June 2003

#1 Best City for Education
—*Places Rated Almanac*, Millennium Edition

Index

CORWIN PRESS

The Corwin Press logo—a raven striding across an open book—represents the union of courage and learning. Corwin Press is committed to improving education for all learners by publishing books and other professional development resources for those serving the field of PreK–12 education. By providing practical, hands-on materials, Corwin Press continues to carry out the promise of its motto: **"Helping Educators Do Their Work Better."**